Civic Studies

Civic Studies

Edited by Peter Levine and Karol Edward Sołtan
Bringing Theory to Practice
Washington, DC

1818 R Street, NW, Washington, DC 20009

ISBN 978-0-9853088-2-7

Civic Studies

Approaches to the emerging field

EDITORS: Peter Levine and Karol Edward Sołtan

CIVIC SERIES EDITOR: Barry Checkoway

CONTENTS

Foreword   viii

Preface   ix

Acknowledgments   xi

PART 1   Overview

Chapter 1   The Case for Civic Studies   3
              Peter Levine

Chapter 2   The Emerging Field of a New Civics   9
              Karol Edward Sołtan

PART 2   The Art and Science of Association: The Bloomington School

Chapter 3   Artisans of the Common Life: Building a Public Science of Civics   23
              Filippo Sabetti

Chapter 4   Citizenship, Political Competence, and Civic Studies:
              The Ostromian Perspective   33
              Paul Dragos Aligica

PART 3   Deliberative Participation

Chapter 5   Deliberative Civic Engagement:
Connecting Public Voices to Public Governance   49
Tina Nabatchi and Greg Munno

Chapter 6   The Challenge of Promoting Civic Participation in Poor Countries   59
Ghazala Mansuri and Vijayendra Rao

PART 4   Public Work

Chapter 7   Transforming Higher Education in a Larger Context:
The Civic Politics of Public Work   77
Harry C. Boyte and Blase Scarnati

Chapter 8   Citizen-Centered Research for Civic Studies:
Bottom Up, Problem Driven, Mixed Methods, Interdisciplinary   91
Sanford Schram

Chapter 9   Public Sociology, Engaged Research, and Civic Education   103
Philip Nyden

Contributors   115
Bringing Theory to Practice   116

FOREWORD

If a "new civics" were to arise in higher education, what would it be?

Colleges and universities are anchor institutions that often express a civic purpose and are, at a time when society is changing in its social characteristics, ideally situated for addressing questions like this. Indeed, it is possible to imagine a campus with a vibrant civic culture—a campus where students engage in curricular and cocurricular activities with a strong civic purpose, where faculty members organize their research and teaching in ways that contribute to the public good, and where the president and provost speak strongly about this work as a driving force for the educational mission. Imagine everyone—from philosophy to physics and from engineering to business—buzzing about how to infuse the new civics into their work, both on campus and in the community. For example, if society is not getting the knowledge it needs, how can the university begin to provide it?

Civic Studies represents an effort to stimulate discussion of some of the questions and issues that arise in thinking about this work. Peter Levine and Karol Edward Sołtan have brought together a group of thinkers and authors who share commitment to this purpose, and have enabled them to express their thoughts and make them public.

Civic Studies is the third volume in the Civic Series, a projected five-volume series of monographs intended to engage educators in conversations about the civic mission of higher education. We are indebted to Bringing Theory to Practice for making the series possible, and to Peter and Karol for a work that is well worth the reading.

Barry Checkoway
General Series Editor

PREFACE

The phrase "civic studies" is quite new. A group of scholars coined it in 2007 in a collaborative statement entitled "The New Civic Politics: Civic Theory and Practice for the Future."[1] That document has been the inspiration of the Summer Institute of Civic Studies, which the two of us have taught annually (at first with Stephen Elkin) and which has drawn almost one hundred graduate students, scholars, and practitioners to Tufts University.

Civic studies does not mean civic education, although it should ultimately improve civic education. Instead, in the words of original framework, civic studies is an "emerging intellectual community, a field, and a discipline. Its work is to understand and strengthen civic politics, civic initiatives, civic capacity, civic society, and civic culture."

The framework cites two definitive ideals for the emerging discipline of civic studies: "public spiritedness" (or "commitment to the public good") and "the idea of the citizen as a creative agent." Civic studies is an intellectual community that takes these two ideals seriously. Although new, it draws from several important strands of ongoing research: the Nobel Prize–winning scholarship of Elinor and Vincent Ostrom on managing common assets, deliberative democracy, public work, the study of public participation in development, the idea of social science as practical wisdom or *phronesis,* and community-based research in fields like sociology. In this volume, each of these strands is represented by one or more leading scholars. By putting their work together, we hope to contribute to the creation of a diverse but robust intellectual community.

Peter Levine and Karol Edward Sołtan
Editors

NOTE

1. Harry Boyte, Stephen Elkin, Peter Levine, Jane Mansbridge, Elinor Ostrom, Karol Sołtan, and Rogers Smith, "The New Civic Politics: Civic Theory and Practice for the Future," framing statement of the Summer Institute of Civic Studies, September 28, 2007, http://activecitizen.tufts.edu/circle/summer-institute/summer-institute-of-civic-studies-framing-statement.

ACKNOWLEDGMENTS

The editors acknowledge Bringing Theory to Practice (BTtoP) and all the supporters of the Civic Series. Special thanks to Dylan Joyce, BTtoP project associate, for his extraordinarily dedicated and careful support throughout the editorial process; to series editor Barry Checkoway, who made the project possible; and to David Tritelli and Liz Clark for editing and design.

We thank colleagues who have been essential to the development of "civic studies," including our fellow authors of the framing statement that first defined this emerging field in 2007: Harry Boyte (University of Minnesota), Stephen Elkin (University of Maryland), Jane Mansbridge (Harvard University) the late and much lamented Elinor Ostrom (Indiana University), and Rogers Smith (University of Pennsylvania).

Also essential to the early progress of civic studies have been the roughly one hundred alumni of the Summer Institute of Civic Studies at the Jonathan M. Tisch College of Citizenship and Public Service at Tufts University, which Stephen Elkin co-founded with us. These graduate students, professors, and seasoned practitioners have contributed their thoughts and passions to help build the field.

Peter Levine and Karol Edward Soltan
Editors

ABOUT THE EDITORS

Peter Levine is Lincoln Filene Professor of Citizenship and Public Affairs and director of CIRCLE (the Center for Information and Research on Civic Learning and Engagement) at Tufts University's Jonathan M. Tisch College of Citizenship and Public Service. He is the author most recently of *We Are the Ones We Have Been Waiting For: The Promise of Civic Renewal in America* (2013).

Karol Edward Soltan teaches political science at the University of Maryland. He has published widely on the civic perspective, moderation, constitutionalism, and political economy. He has worked for the United Nations in East Timor, and as a constitutional adviser to Kurdistan (among other roles). He is writing a book with the tentative title *Civic Moderation*.

Levine and Soltan are codirectors and cofounders of the Summer Institute of Civic Studies at Tufts University.

PART 1 | # Overview

The Case for Civic Studies

1

Peter Levine

I AM GOING TO ASSUME THAT YOU ARE A CITIZEN. I do not mean someone who possesses legal rights and responsibilities in relation to a particular government, but rather a member of one or more communities that you want to improve. Your communities may range from a block of houses or a single church to the whole earth. You want to address these communities' problems and influence their directions, but more than that, you want to *make* them through your work, your thought, your passion. You want to be a co-creator of your worlds.

For you, scholarship—advanced intellectual work—ought to be a resource. With more than 300,000 different new books published in the United States every year (not to mention articles, websites, old books, and works from overseas), you can surely find valuable texts to read. And yet, overwhelmingly, scholarship is *not* addressed to you as a citizen.

On the whole, today's scholarship is most valuable as a source of facts. And you do need facts to be an active and responsible citizen. What causes the disease that is assaulting your community? What cures it? How much would the cure cost? If the government raised taxes to provide the cure, what would happen to the unemployment rate?

The social, behavioral, and medical sciences present themselves as providers of such empirical information, including both descriptive facts and causal facts. You can look up the results in scientific journals and books.

Almost all students of these disciplines are taught that truth is elusive because the observer has biases. One should work hard to overcome or minimize biases, using elaborate techniques for that purpose (conducting double-blind clinical trials, for example, or achieving agreement among many observers). But since such efforts will never fully succeed, social scientists are told to disclose and acknowledge their biases as limitations or caveats. They then present the facts as best they can.

Once they say what they believe is true, their readers are supposed to apply values to decide what ought to be done. For instance, unemployment is bad; it would be worth spending billions to lower unemployment. These two value propositions are not themselves results of social science. Citizens must bring values into the discussion because social scientists do not claim special expertise about values.

Once we put facts together with values, we can make recommendations for society. And once we have recommendations, we can act effectively—or hope that someone else acts—to improve society.

That is the implicit, standard model. It is widely taught in graduate and professional schools. It explains how most scholars approach social issues and the division of labor in their disciplines. But the standard model presents a host of problems, some well known and some a little subtler.

First, purported facts are always imbued with norms. Education, for example, is related to employment—but what is education? The average number of years that people spend in school looks like a hard number, an objective fact, but no one believes it's worth measuring unless it is a proxy for education, rightly understood. The real definition of education is some process that enhances human flourishing. Thus measuring education requires a theory of the human good. According to the standard model taught to social scientists, moral theories are just biases or opinions held by ordinary citizens that should be disclosed as biases if they influence scientists. But to call a theory of human flourishing a mere opinion or bias is to deny the difference between right and wrong. What we need is a *good* theory of the human good.

> *A citizen needs knowledge of rights and wrongs, facts and explanations, and strategies. The citizen should be accountable for all of that: explaining what she believes and why. Her strategies must include the citizen herself*

That brings me to the second criticism of the standard theory. It assumes that values are opinions, tastes, preferences, or biases. But moral assertions can be right or wrong. I am sitting on a chair; I must not kill a random stranger for fun. Both statements are right. The methods we use to know right from wrong are controversial, but it's easy to see that some opinions about values are contemptibly wrong: not just Mussolini's or Chairman Mao's, but the opinions of everyday people who happily waste more than they create, burden society and the earth, and sow more sorrow than joy. To say that morality is a mere matter of opinion is to deny the existence of vice and evil.

We certainly do not experience making moral decisions as a matter of preferences or opinions, like choosing a flavor of ice cream. We feel that we are striving to make the right choices, to reach objectively the right conclusions, regardless of our own preferences and tastes. If that feeling is meaningful at all, then moral reflection must be some kind of inquiry into truth.

Third, empirical information influences norms. The fact that we can have reasonably stable democratic governments is an essential reason that we *ought* to have democratic governments. We have learned from experience, not only what works but what is important and attractive. If I thought we could revolutionize or abolish the family to enhance justice for children, I'd be interested in that idea, but I'd need a lot more examples of success before the pure philosophical argument became attractive. Most people think that "ought implies can": if there is a moral obligation to do something, that act must be possible. I would add that, sometimes, "can implies ought": if something has been demonstrated to work well, we are obligated to do it. This is another way in which facts and values are intertwined.

Fourth, strategic considerations rightly influence norms. We might propose that everyone has a right to a job. I would agree with that. But then I owe an explanation of how everyone can be afforded a job without very bad effects on the economy, freedom, or work itself. And it's not enough to say that a government could enact a particular package of reforms that would achieve that end. I must also ask what would cause an actual government to act in helpful ways. My statement that "everyone has a right to a job" could help if it proved persuasive. Or my statement could be unhelpful. It might gain no traction, provoke a public backlash, divide an existing political coalition, or lead to a massive new government program that does not work. Depending on the situation, I might do better advocating a particular reform in the welfare system that has a real prospect of passage. Unless I have a plan for getting everyone a job, my statement that everyone has a right to a job may be worse than no theory at all.

Fifth, strategy and values influence empirical evidence. For instance, how do we get the employment statistics that we have? They are not generated automatically. People struggled to persuade government agencies to collect certain job-related data. Those agencies defined "unemployment" so that you are unemployed if you once held a full-time job, were laid off, and are actively seeking employment, but not if you left high school to help raise your young sister. The definition of unemployment reflects choices that people struggle over—not only in their heads and on paper, but by taking political action to change what is measured. Meanwhile, other information is not available at all. In short, our values and strategic actions influence even the data we possess.

A citizen needs knowledge of rights and wrongs, facts and explanations, *and* strategies. The citizen should be accountable for all of that: explaining what she believes and why. Her strategies must include the citizen herself. For example, it is not a strategy to say that the government should provide vaccines for everyone. That is a wish. A strategy would explain how we—you and I—can get the government to provide those vaccines. It is also essential that the vaccines *work* (that is the factual part) and that they make human lives *better* (the values). Again, all three strands must be integrated, because there is just one fundamental question: What should you and I do?

I wrote "you and I" instead of just "I" because purely individual actions are usually ineffective, and also for a deeper reason—because the good life is lived in common. Toddlers demonstrate "parallel play," sitting side-by-side but doing their own thing. With maturity comes the ability to play together, to decide together what to play, to learn from the other players, to bring new players into the game, and to make up new games. That is what we do when we are co-creators of a common world. Not only are the results better, but we lead deeper and richer lives when we strive together.

Scholarship is not well organized to serve people who see themselves as citizens, meaning co-creators of their common worlds. The disciplines that assume there may be a real difference between right and wrong (philosophy, political theory, theology, and some other portions of the humanities) are rigidly separated from the disciplines that deal with purported facts. The professional schools teach strategies to prospective business leaders, lawyers, and doctors, but no department teaches strategies for citizens. Philosophy addresses the nature of justice but not what actions available to you and to me might make the world more just. According to the official definition of the American Political Science Association, "Political science is the study of governments, public policies and political processes, systems, and political behavior."[1] It is not an investigation of what you and I should do together. That question was a traditional topic for "civics" class, but civics was always restricted to K-12 schools and is now being replaced even there by courses that mimic college-level political science. The proportion of American high school students who take a government class has been essentially flat since 1915, whereas courses labeled "civics" or "problems of democracy," once common, are now almost gone.[2]

Meanwhile, scholars often hold a peculiar stance toward practice. Consider the example of an educational strategy, such as asking students to conduct community service as part of their courses. This practice, known as "service learning," may be especially familiar to readers of the Civic Series, but the same analysis would apply to medical treatments or welfare programs—to any body or field of practice that involves human beings. The standard scholarly stance is to determine whether the practice "works" by collecting and analyzing evidence of impact. If the practice does work, the scholarly findings can arm practitioners with favorable evidence, persuade policymakers to invest in it, and contribute to general knowledge. If the practice doesn't work, the scholarship implies that it should stop. Scholarly authors do not disclose their feelings of hope, satisfaction, or disappointment when they publish their results.

But if service learning "works," why would that be so? Surely because dedicated practitioners stuck with the idea even in the face of evidence that it was *not* successful in the early attempts and improved their methods. For them, service learning was not a hypothesis to be tested and rejected if proved wrong. It was a practice that embodied empirical, strategic, and value assumptions. Perhaps the practitioners hoped to engage students in service because they were communitarians who believe that the good life requires close and caring interactions. Or perhaps they sought economic equality and hoped to boost the job prospects of disadvantaged youth by engaging them in service. No doubt, their commitments varied, but they built a community of practitioners with some loyalty to each other and whose actual methods have evolved. Their commitments and the community they produced are fundamental; the methods and outcomes constantly shift.

Scholars of service learning can be understood as part of the same community. Like the practitioners, the scholars are motivated by core beliefs. They have not randomly selected service learning as an "intervention" to assess; they *hope* that it will work because it reflects their commitments. They study it in order to build a case for it while also providing constructive feedback to the practitioners, with whom they have formed working relationships. When they get negative results, their loyalty keeps them looking for solutions. All of this is perfectly healthy, except that the scholars' hope, loyalty, and other emotions and values are not considered scientific, so they leave them out of their professional writing. Most research on service learning makes it sound like a laboratory experiment.

The authors of this volume see civic studies as a strategy for reorienting academic scholarship so that it does address citizens—and learns from them in turn. In fact, it treats scholars *as* citizens who are engaged with others in creating their worlds. Civic studies integrates facts, values, and strategies. Those who practice this nascent discipline are accountable to the public for what they believe to be true, to be good, and to work. They are accountable for the actual results of their thoughts and not just the ideas themselves.

Civic studies is a large river fed by tributaries of scholars and practitioners who share commitments to particular forms of civic action in the world.

For many centuries, people have been successfully managing common resources such as forests and fish stocks, even though a simplistic theory of human interaction would suggest that people will act in their individual self-interest and use them up. The late Elinor and Vincent Ostrom and their students, often known as the "Bloomington School," studied how citizens successfully manage common goods. They learned from practical experience and contributed sophisticated political theory and formal modeling of human interactions; indeed, Elinor Ostrom won the Nobel Prize in economics. They developed practical guidance for citizens who try to manage common goods. They had an implicit moral framework in which good citizenship meant overcoming collective-action problems. In this volume, the chapters by Filippo Sabetti (chapter 3) and Paul Dragos Aligica (chapter 4) describe and develop this first stream of work.

For as long as they have been managing common resources, people have been deliberating about public issues. Deliberative democracy is a field of practice that encourages such discussions, strives to make them fair and equal, and connects the outcomes to government decisions. Tina Nabatchi and Greg Munno exemplify scholars who study and practice public deliberation (chapter 5). Governments can also promote and encourage deliberative input by citizens, and Ghazala Mansur and Vijayendra Rao devote chapter 6 to that kind of public participation as a field of practice and research.

Public work can be introduced as a partial critique of deliberative democracy. It insists that citizens should not only talk and render judgments but actually work and make things as part of their citizenship. Put a different way, it views work sites and work identities as central to citizenship. Another stream of practice and research, it is represented in this volume by Harry Boyte and Blase Scarnati (chapter 7).

The Danish planning professor Bent Flyvbjerg shook up social science when he argued that the search for general, predictive rules was a "wasteful dead end."[3] Instead, social scientists should display "practical reason" (*phronesis*) in collaboration with laypeople. Sanford Schram's chapter 8 is a defense of social science as *phronesis,* another stream that feeds civic studies. Not too different is public sociology as described in chapter 9 by Philip Nyden, who is also a leading practitioner of Community-Based Participatory Research (CBPR).

Common-pool resource management, deliberation, public participation, public work, social science as *phronesis,* public sociology, and CBPR—these are fruitfully different and even opposed on certain issues. But they all take the perspective of the citizen, draw on and enrich practical experience, and aim for a combination of facts, values, and strategies. Out of these streams, civic studies is forming.

NOTES

1. "What is Political Science?," American Political Science Association, accessed October 7, 2013, https://www.apsanet.org/content_9181.cfm. For context, see James W. Ceasar, *The Role of Political Science and Political Scientists in Civic Education* (Washington, DC: American Enterprise Institute, 2013), http://www.aei.org/files/2013/08/07/-the-role-of-political-science-and-political -scientists-in-civic-education_161230853228.pdf.

2. Richard G. Niemi and Julia Smith, "Enrollments in High School Government Classes: Are We Short-Changing Both Citizenship and Political Science Training?," *PS: Political Science and Politics* 34, no. 2 (2001): 282. For updated data, see Mark Hugo Lopez, Karlo Barrios Marcelo, and Peter Levine, *Getting Narrower at the Base: The American Curriculum After NCLB,* (Medford, MA: Center for Information & Research on Civic Learning & Engagement, 2008), www.civicyouth.org/PopUps/Narrowing_Curriculum.pdf.

3. Bent Fylybjerg, "Social Science that Matters," *Foresight Europe* (October/March 2006): 38.

2 | The Emerging Field of a New Civics

Karol Edward Sołtan

CIVIC STUDIES (or "the new civics," as I will sometimes call it) is an emerging field whose goal is to develop ideas and ways of thinking that are helpful to citizens understood as co-creators of their worlds. This much is broadly agreed. Explaining some of the possible meanings of this goal would be a good way to introduce the new field. But before I do that, let me suggest a second goal, namely, to make a significant intellectual contribution to those outside this intellectual community, to unsettle and transform the wider culture in order to make it more supportive of human beings as co-creators. What larger culture? The new civics ought not to be provincial, so the larger culture we may hope to change is most broadly the global modern culture in its various embodiments around the world.

The term "citizen" can mean a variety of things. In one context it refers to a form of membership in a group, with its associated rights and duties. More narrowly it refers to membership in a state. There is a large literature on citizenship understood in this state-centered way, but it is not the literature of civic studies (although there is an overlap). The rights and duties of citizenship is not our subject, except incidentally. So what is?

Consider the simple exercise of dropping the word "citizen" entirely from the goal of this emerging field. Civic studies, we could say, aims to develop ideas and ways of thinking helpful to human beings in their capacity as co-creators of their worlds. I think that would be a good start. To co-create is jointly to bring something into existence. But this can happen over time and in stages. We help create something when we modify it. But only certain kinds of modification count, not destruction or damage. We help create something when we improve it. On some days, I am convinced that all human creation really is creation together and that, in that sense, our subject simply is human creation. But I will not insist on this. The creativity of great individual geniuses certainly is distinctive, even if they work on material created by others, and are deeply dependent on such material.

> *Civic studies, we could say, aims to develop ideas and ways of thinking helpful to human beings in their capacity as co-creators of their worlds*

Our subject is human beings as co-creators, agents who help improve their worlds. It is not human beings as spectators, or as victims or puppets of forces beyond their control, or as very complex machines. The human mind is creative. We act. We take initiatives. And the greatest products of this creative activity require us to create together with others, to co-create. We are then co-creators of our worlds. And, in the broadest sense of the word, we are citizens. Certainly citizens of a democratic state are called, at least sometimes, to act together. But for civic studies, the relevant image and the relevant inspiration is not so much the citizen of a democratic state, as a society full of civic initiatives. We might call it "civic society" (a more accurate term for what is often called "civil society").

But what is really distinctive and challenging about civic studies is that it aims to develop ideas that would be *helpful* to this process of co-creation. And if an idea is helpful to the process, then we can see that idea as being a *part* of that process. So the field of civic studies aims to study human co-creation by participating in it.

Does that mean that all the work in civic studies must address the public directly? Scholars in many fields have made an effort to address the public directly. Public sociology, for example, is a form of sociology that aims to address the public (see chapter 9). There are political scientists who also aspire to speak to the public directly. In both cases, these efforts lie outside the mainstream and represent an attempt to reform these fields by making them less isolated from the world, more engaged and relevant. Such efforts make it hard to develop abstract and complex arguments or theories, however. The price paid is that one cannot be too intellectually ambitious or deep. Certainly some thinkers and scholars in civic studies speak to the public directly in this way as well. But the goal is to develop ideas that would be *helpful* to co-creators, which one can do without addressing those co-creators directly. We should expect the development of complex and abstract theories in civic studies. Civic studies is intellectually serious in a way civic practitioners need not be. A civic studies curriculum is full of high-level theory; it makes no intellectual compromises.

Venues and social potential

The statement of our goal goes further. We aim to develop ideas that would be helpful to *co-creators* of their *worlds*. What does that mean? Let me work backward in explaining this. First, what do we mean by worlds? Second, how should we understand co-creation? With regard to "worlds," the plural is crucial. We all live in one shared world. But speaking metaphorically, we also all live in many worlds that we share with different people—the "worlds" of family, work, and organizations, but also other more fleeting worlds that we enter and leave constantly. In discussing these worlds, I will use the terms "venues" and "situations" interchangeably. A co-creator approaches a venue in a distinctive way, looking for how it can be improved. So we will need to develop a correspondingly distinctive practical account of venues and of ways to improve those venues (practical, because intended to help action).

The venues or situations in which distinctive kinds of civic work can occur may be fleeting and small scale, like negotiations or deliberations, or they may be large and important, like the sovereign territorial states that dominate the world or like the world (singular) itself. The world is the most inclusive setting for civic work, but the possible venues of civic work are quite varied. They can include universities, corporations, communities and neighborhoods, social movements, the Internet, favelas, prisons, and civil wars.

What would it mean to do civic work in such venues? It would mean working together to help make them better places. We must be able to distinguish better from worse. We must be able to bring to bear ideals that are not arbitrary. Without that we cannot make the world a better place. We must explore more broadly the social potential of a given venue and the ways in which it could be improved. Community organizations do that, and they frequently begin by doing two things. It is helpful to know what in a given situation is possible, what is difficult, and what might be made easy. So, first, community organizations try to outline a power map of the venue: who are the players, what are the relationships among the players, what resources do they have access to, and what resources can be brought into play? Second, they try to explore what we might call the local culture of the venue: what ideas and ideals are prominent, what do people believe and value, what are they are serious about, what could they be convinced to be serious about, and in what way do they think their world can be improved? It is best to do this through deliberation. So deliberation can be a crucial instrument for the exploration of the social potential of a situation. Deliberation takes many forms and can have many goals—to improve decisions, to show all affected equal respect, to build consensus.[1] There are many ways to promote or assist with deliberation. For example, one of the important theoretical frameworks in civic studies, social science as phronesis (described in chapter 8), is in effect an effort to develop a social science capable of exploring the social potential of situations. It aims to contribute to deliberation.

More generally, we can also help deliberation by studying its various forms in order to determine which are best suited to the discovery of social potential in a given situation—to determine, for example, how to avoid the most common distortions and defects of deliberation as a process of discovery. We need to know not only what might be the ideal forms of deliberation for this purpose, but also what practical alternatives are the best approximations to the ideal. In different settings, these explorations will take different forms. When the situation is more like a fleeting negotiation, the exploration of social potential looks more like what Roger Fisher and William Ury call "principled negotiation."[2] There are many alternatives to explore here.

Civic studies can be described as a science of social potential. And when we think like global citizens, we are exploring the social potential of the human situation most generally, what can be called human potential. Others prefer to use different terminology. Perhaps the most popular is the language of problem solving: we identify and define problems, and then help solve them. We develop problem-oriented or solution-oriented social science, as discussed by Sanford Schram (chapter 8) and Philip Nyden (chapter 9) in this volume. Yet I would argue that a situation's potential for improvement is not always best described as a "problem" to be solved.

CREATION AND DIFFICULTY

Let me turn now to my second topic. How should we think more systematically about human co-creation, in a way that would be helpful to co-creation? Social science has a natural inclination to search for causal explanations of human action. When we succeed in constructing such an explanation, we present the actions we explain as *determined* by the causes. Human creativity disappears. And if we construct an explanation with a probabilistic component, then there is room for randomness and chance, but still not for human creativity. In response to this tendency in social science, we now have a large and distinguished literature consisting of efforts to leave a space in our accounts of human action for voluntary action, for human initiative and creativity, for what is often called "human agency."

Proponents of civic studies promise to do something more intellectually radical. We are not satisfied with views that *allow* for human creativity; we seek instead to develop views that *help* this creativity. In this way, we also study the process of creation in a very intimate way, from the inside. Our ideas are part of the process.

How to proceed? It is too early in the development of the field for any kind of consensus to have emerged, or even for the issues to be clear. But let me propose the following: the key is the idea of *difficulty*. If you are used to social scientific thinking, you will say that difficulty is the central variable. And if you are used to more formal ways of thinking, you will say that to each imaginable outcome (or action or event), we need to associate two numbers: one to measure the difficulty of obtaining the outcome, and one to measure the difficulty of avoiding the outcome. If the difficulty of *obtaining* the outcome is extreme, that outcome is impossible. If the difficulty of *avoiding* the outcome is extreme, that outcome is inevitable (or necessary). A world of such extreme difficulty is a world of the impossible and the inevitable, and hence a world in which there is no room for human creative activity or voluntary action. Human creation emerges as we succeed in diminishing difficulty. In the process, we turn what was initially impossible into something that is merely difficult, and then we reduce this difficulty further.

This way of thinking about the process of human creation suggests a way of organizing our ideas in order to be helpful to this process. We need to identify the sources of difficulty—let us call them impediments—and ways of diminishing their force. Many of the most important theorists in the canon of civic studies can be read as doing just that. Elinor Ostrom (together with others) identifies the problem of collective action as a key impediment and studies ways of overcoming it.[3] Her work is a central inspiration of chapters 3 and 4 of this volume. Jürgen Habermas is concerned with how in the modern world what he calls "the life world" (a world of spontaneous interactions and conversations) is distorted and colonized by what he calls the "system" (roughly: power based on threats and promises). Distortions are the impediment, and Habermas looks for ways to diminish their effect.[4] Practical experiments in deliberative democracy, emphasized in chapter 5, have been inspired by Habermas. Friedrich Hayek, Karl Popper, and many others identify limited human cognitive capacity as the key impediment, and find in many modern institutions the necessary adaptations to that impediment: division of labor, decentralization, error prevention mechanisms such as deliberation, and error correction mechanisms such as are found in markets and in the democratic requirement of free periodic election to high office.[5]

Let us consider in more detail two additional sources of difficulty that represent key challenges to the task of co-creation: human moral limits and the difficulty of preserving continuity in our efforts to make the world better.

HUMAN MORAL LIMITS

Perhaps the two most important ways in which the new civics must challenge established ways of thinking are, first, through its aim to be helpful to the human being as co-creator, and, second, through the way we take seriously human ideals. The new civics would fit nicely into the intellectual establishment if it weren't for the field's insistence that human beings are not spectators, machines, puppets, or victims. Human beings are agents, and they are best understood as such through ideas and ways of thinking that help them in their agency. We would also fit in nicely if we thought we could help co-creators only in their choice of means, if we were to limit ourselves to exercises in instrumental rationality. But perhaps the greater need is in the development of ends and ultimate principles. We do not want to see citizens pursue with great rationality ends that are mad or deluded or evil.

Many of the authors who belong in the theoretical canon of civic studies either explicitly think of themselves as combining social science and philosophy, or can be seen as doing so. Jürgen Habermas, Bent Flyvbjerg, Roberto Mangabeira Unger, and Philip Selznick come to mind as examples. For the most part, they turn to philosophy out of a need to develop a well-articulated and well-defended normative perspective, including ends and ultimate principles. But we might be disappointed if we follow their example. Political philosophy and ethics have a long history of development as professional disciplines separate from the great and small projects of humanity. Philosophers mostly read and engage other philosophers. They can sometimes seem far away from the front lines of the articulation of defensible ideals for ongoing civic projects.

The human moral limitations most relevant to the task of co-creation can be summarized in a brief sentence: human ideals are vague, distorted, and weak. So we have three crucial moral impediments. To combat vagueness, we need to articulate ideals and help them become real guides to action. To diminish distorting forces, we need to identify those forces and help create conditions that weaken them. We can draw here on Habermas's theory of communicative ethics and deliberation.[6] But Habermas will not help us much with the fundamental problem of weak moral motivation.

Our moral motivation, the influence of ideals on what we do, can be strengthened when those ideals are embedded in projects that look promising (they might actually change the world). Then, our idealism is not wasted—and a scandalous amount of human idealism *is* wasted. Above all, we search for and articulate ideals that inspire us. A notable contemporary example is the principle of the inviolability of human dignity, which is at the heart of the project of universal human rights. Again and again, this principle has proven its capacity to inspire. But philosophers have been extremely reluctant to take it seriously. Only in the last few years has this changed. But still, the most promising efforts to articulate (make less vague) this principle come from practitioners of international law, not philosophy. I have in mind, for example, Andrew Clapham's identification of four dimensions of human dignity: the integrity of the body, equal respect, a social and economic minimum, and protection of sources of meaning, such as religion.[7]

The problem of continuity and renewable projects

We can approach the task of civic work in a venue by first exploring its social potential in the manner I suggest above. This runs the risk of producing disjointed civic initiatives, however; there may be improvements, but they will not add up. There will be little continuity over time, and little chance of producing deep and sustained change. Consider the much repeated civic parable of the two bricklayers. The first bricklayer thought of himself as building a wall. His heart was not in it, but he had to do what he had to do—the bare required minimum. The second bricklayer thought of herself as part of a larger and more significant project—she was building a temple. She was inspired and motivated. Civic initiatives may be just isolated walls, or they can add up to a temple. But they do need to add up. One initiative needs to build on another; there has to be some continuity. Ideally, individual civic initiatives are parts of larger, ongoing, shared projects. The grandest and most significant examples of human co-creation involve not only the cooperation of individuals across what we might call social space. They also involve the cooperation of individuals across time. We build on what we inherit from previous generations, and we make a gift of what we build to future generations.

Shared projects are a form of creative social capital. The term "capital," originally used in economics, can refer to any stock that produces a valuable flow. In the first instance, it refers to the stock of machines used in a factory to make valuable products. By extension, it is often helpful to speak of *human* capital when referring to those skills and traits of an individual that produce for him or her a valuable flow of actions and outcomes. Environmentalists draw our attention to *natural* capital, elements of our natural environment that produce a valuable flow, and we now also have a large literature on *social* capital, all those things individuals share—such as the relationships between them and their shared institutions—that produce for them a valuable flow. Robert Putnam famously developed an account that links certain forms of social capital to the valuable ongoing capacity to work together (i.e., to overcome the problem of collective action), and to a broad range of valuable outcomes.[8]

Shared projects are, I say, a form of *social* capital. They are a stock that produces a valuable flow of continuing improvements, continuing creation, innovation, invention, and reform. And they are shared, hence, creative social capital.

We can expect that co-creation (civic work) relying on projects will produce a pattern of development following roughly a logistic curve, and that we will be able to identify distinctive stages. Initially, we see little innovation because creative effort is concentrated on building the project itself (the "stock," the equivalent of the factory machine). Once the project is ready, we will expect to see a burst of reforms and innovations. But projects are not inexhaustible capital. Eventually, their potential for innovation starts running out and progress slows down.

This pattern suggests that projects by themselves are not a long-term solution to the problem of continuity. As a project is exhausted, continuity is at risk of being broken. But it need not be. As a project nears the crisis of its own exhaustion, it can be reformulated in a novel way that preserves continuity even as it establishes new potential for improvement. Here scientific research programs or paradigms are perhaps the best examples. As the Newtonian paradigm was exhausted, it was reformulated in the theory of relativity and in quantum physics. The new version of the project builds on the old, but it also profoundly transforms it. The problem of continuity can be solved by projects with a capacity for renewal. In our example, the Newtonian project was exhausted, but the larger project of physical science was renewed and flourished.

How should we understand such projects, this stock that produces a valuable flow? What are their essential elements and organization? In the new civics, we should understand them from the perspective of those who rely on this shared stock (this social capital) to help them create. A good starting point is what we might call the canon of the project. What should we teach to those who will participate in the development of a project? To sustain itself, a project must have a canon; it must be capable of being taught to those who will take part in its development. Such a canon would include the basic elements of a practical account of the project.

Projects in the form of scientific research programs, or programs of technological development, each have their distinct canons. Projects that support social and political reform do as well. They should include, I would suggest, at least the following: a code of principles or ideals (and debates about that code); an institutional repertoire to sustain and develop the institutional imagination (and debates about institutions); a strategic repertoire to sustain and develop the strategic imagination (and debates about strategy); a collection of inspiring exemplars (and perhaps counter-exemplars to teach us what to avoid); a civic history (crucial to maintain continuity); testing methods to evaluate initiatives; and—finally—background knowledge and research programs. As part of the background knowledge, we should include an understanding of the most important impediments to co-creation and what we know about how to overcome them. Civic studies aims to develop these essential components of civic projects.

The canon of a project can be organized into what we might call levels. We have, first, the canon for the protection and maintenance of the project. We have, next, the canon for everyday improvement. And we have, finally, the canon for the transformative stage. The latter may be only intermittently *necessary*, only in periods of crisis and exhaustion. But there is also a way of avoiding what we might call the cycle of creation—a pattern of development that is made up, roughly, of a sequence of logistic curves or periods of development separated by periods of crisis. We can avoid this cycle if we incorporate the capacity for renewal more permanently into our projects, thereby making them capable of a kind of permanent renaissance.

So we can expect to understand a project at three levels, and perhaps also to develop three levels of civic education supportive of a project. The first would aim to maintain and defend the project, the second would support routine improvements, and the third would look for deeper transformation.[9]

I have illustrated, I hope, some of the potential of the new civics. It explores the social potential of venues large and small, and it develops practical theories of projects large and small. It searches for how venues without projects can be improved, even if only in a disjointed way, and it helps with venues that are defined by ongoing projects—including big projects such as the American project (or the French, the Chinese, the Mexican or Ethiopian projects, some of them ancient), the project of modernity, and the encompassing global project. The latter is of special importance; it is the subject matter of global civics, the most encompassing subfield of the emerging field of the new civics.

GLOBAL CIVICS

Global civics, understood as an emerging intellectual community, has as its goal the development of ideas and ways of thinking that can be helpful to human beings in their capacity as co-creators of the world. Its concern is with humanity's most encompassing project, with the human situation as a whole.

Such a comprehensive project is distinctive insofar as it includes all the other projects, and all the others are included in it. So the canon of this comprehensive project should be included in the canon of all projects. This comprehensive project, a way of doing civic work globally in the venue of the human situation in general, is the civic form of the dream of a united and flourishing humanity. It amounts to an effort to make the ideals of that dream less vague, less distorted, and stronger, and to turn the dream into a promising project.

This encompassing project is not purely global. It aims to incorporate and support all other projects that deserve our help—including not only the smallest of such projects, most notably those of each individual human life, but also the vast mosaic of shared projects that deserve our loyalty or, at least, our recognition.

Have we, in fact, inherited such a truly encompassing project, a project that includes or, perhaps, supports (in the manner of an incubator) all projects that deserve our help? Can we build on what we have inherited? It seems so. This project has a long past that reaches back most notably to the goal of uniting All-Under-Heaven, a goal that was first formulated in ancient China.[10] It also has a complex history in more recent times. We can "start" in the nineteenth century with initiatives to constrain and limit war (resulting in the two International Peace Conferences in Hague in 1899 and 1907). The two world wars of the twentieth century dramatically intensified interest in the project. And in the brief period between World War II and the Cold War, there was an extraordinary awakening of interest in the global project. This interest was expressed through political and institutional initiatives (the United Nations, the World Bank, the International Monetary Fund, the beginnings of the unification of Europe), as well as a great wave of intellectual innovation, thinking through (for example) the long-term history of the aspiration to a universal civilization. The Cold War discouraged and narrowed the focus of these initiatives almost exclusively to the question of avoiding war.

After the Cold War, interest in the global project reemerged and has been rein-forced by growing economic globalization and social interdependence. But we have seen fewer of the kind of theoretical contributions that made the 1940s so amazing.

The intellectual juices are once again stirring in the various disciplines—espe-cially normative international relations, international law, and, to a somewhat lesser degree, economics, philosophy, and sociology. As is the case with respect to the new civics as a whole, the strength of disciplinary boundaries—and, perhaps especially, the relative isolation of international law—has made it difficult for an intellectual community to emerge.

What would we teach through a curriculum on global civics? Drawing on the work of Hakan Altinay and his collaborators (with notable additions from inter-national law),[11] I would suggest the following. First, we would consider the emerging codes of principles in the global realm. Some of them either are or could soon become "soft global law." They are written into documents—like the Uni-versal Declaration of Human Rights and the Earth Charter—that, although they lack the authority of law, have the authority of a shared vision.

Second, we would present currently available institutional arrangements rel-evant to the global project—those of global and regional institutions that are part of globalization from above, as well as those of institutions such as the civic organizations of the "global civil society" that are part of globalization from below. Third, we would introduce the debates concerning institutional reform and strategy as well as the debates about the great issues of the day—development, trade and investment, human rights and justice, peace and security, ecological sustainability and ecological renewal. We would consider the most important theoretical traditions in global civics that center around cosmopolitan democracy, the global constitution, and global justice. And we would gain from the integra-tion of global civics into the larger civics, taking full account, for example, of the impediments to co-creation that need to be diminished in order to give promise to this as to any other project.

CONCLUDING COMMENTS

Part of the task of the new civics is to develop more generalized learning about co-creation, to make it possible to learn from multiple different venues of co-creation and from the development of different projects. Another part of the task is to construct as complete a list as possible of significant impediments to creation and ways to diminish their impact. Especially at the beginning of the development of the field, we will need to bring together many narrower perspectives—scholars who specialize in one type of venue or project or in one kind of impediment.

The new civics is emerging out of a clash of ideas and perspectives, including eunomics, constitutional thinking, critical social theory as a rational recon-struction of the conditions of possibility of human emancipation, social science as phronesis, and public work. Its development is being shaped by lessons learned from many civic initiatives in diverse venues, including community organizing, deliberative initiatives, color revolutions (the peaceful efforts to undermine dic-tatorships that became such a common model after 1989), and efforts to build a global civic society.

The new civics has multiple inspirations. It builds on past efforts to create an art and science of association and a science of legislation. It is a response both to Alexander Hamilton's (1787) challenge in *The Federalist* no. 1 to develop "good government based on reflection and choice" and to efforts to build civic societies in the face of communist tyranny—efforts that were, as Vaclav Havel put it, driven by the feeling of responsibility for the world.[12]

Our goal is to create a discipline—an institutionalized intellectual community with a journal, conferences, a professional organization, and a place in the university. We can imagine a fully institutionalized discipline of civic studies based on a network of university centers of civic studies, entities similar but not identical to conventional departments. The goal of these centers would be to promote through research and teaching the development of the discipline of civic studies *and* to support the civic mission of their universities. In addition to providing support for research and teaching, these centers would promote student civic engagement by providing internships and other opportunities as well as support the civic interests of university faculty across the disciplines. The new civics would also be related to what we might call a global movement of civic awakening and renewal. But the most serious goal is intellectual: to unsettle modern culture by the ideas we produce, making it more supportive of human efforts to co-create our worlds—and our world.

NOTES

1. For more detail, see two chapters in this volume: Tina Nabatchi and Greg Munno's chapter 5, "Deliberative Civic Engagement: Connecting Public Voices to Public Governance," and Ghazala Mansuri and Vijayendra Rao's chapter 6, "The Challenge of Promoting Civic Participation in Poor Countries."

2. Roger Fisher and William Ury, *Getting to Yes: Negotiating Agreement Without Giving In* (New York: Penguin Books, 1983), 13.

3. Elinor Ostrom, *Governing the Commons* (Cambridge: Cambridge University Press, 1990); Elinor Ostrom, "Covenants, Collective Action and Common Pool Resources," in *The Constitution of Good Societies*, ed. Karol Edward Sołtan and Stephen Elkin (University Park, PA: Pennsylvania State University Press, 1996), 23–38.

4. Jürgen Habermas, *The Theory of Communicative Action, Volume 2: Lifeworld and System: A Critique of Functionalist Reason,* trans. Thomas McCarthy (Boston: Beacon Press, 1987).

5. Karl Popper, *Open Society and Its Enemies* (New York: Routledge, 1945); Karl Popper, *Conjectures and Refutations* (London: Routledge, 1963); Friedrich Hayek, *The Constitution of Liberty* (Chicago: University of Chicago Press, 1960).

6. Jürgen Habermas, *Moral Consciousness and Communicative Action* (Cambridge, MA: MIT Press, 1990).

7. Andrew Clapham, *Human Rights Obligations of Non-State Actors* (New York: Oxford University Press, 2006): 535-48.

8. Robert D. Putnam, Robert Leonardi, Raffaella Y. Nanetti, *Making Democracy Work: Civic Traditions in Modern Italy* (Princeton, NJ: Princeton University Press, 1992); Robert D. Putnam, *Bowling Alone: The Collapse and Revival of American Community* (New York: Simon and Schuster, 2000).

9. Joel Westheimer and Joseph E. Kahne, "Educating the 'Good Citizen': Political Choices and Pedagogical Goals" *PS* 37, no. 2 (2004): 1–7.

10. Tingyang Zhao "A Political World Philosophy in Terms of All-Under-Heaven (Tian-xia)," *Diogenes* 56, no. 1 (2009): 5–18.

11. Hakan Altinay, ed., *Global Civics* (Washington, DC: Brookings Institution Press, 2011).

12. See especially, Vaclav Havel, *The Art of the Impossible* (New York: Fromm International, 1998): 109–14.

PART 2

The Art
and Science
of Association:
The Bloomington School

Artisans of the Common Life: Building a Public Science of Civics

3

Filippo Sabetti [1]

THIS CHAPTER SEEKS TO GIVE HISTORICAL DEPTH to contemporary recognition of citizens as creative artisans of institutions for collective action. Civic artisanship refers to citizen competence and self-governance, and it takes place when individuals who participate in ongoing patterns of relationships can devise some of their own rules to govern those relationships within particular domains. In uncovering relevant knowledge about self-governance, the chapter broadens the contemporary path toward civic studies.

Why should we bother about the past? We can learn a lot from it. First, ordinary people have for centuries confronted and resolved the challenges of organizing and reorganizing their coexistence in diverse settings—well before modern academics uncovered the logic of collective action in the 1950s and the tragedy of the commons in the 1960s. Second, the problem of organized existence and what gives meaning to individual competence and self-governance is transhistorical. Third, building a public science of civic studies is best viewed as an inter-civilizational phenomenon across space, time, and linguistic communities. Fourth, this chapter suggests how and why the work of Vincent and Elinor Ostrom and, more generally, what has come to be known as the Bloomington School offers a mode of analysis for synthesizing the vast amount of highly specialized historical knowledge that has accumulated, and for mining the archival documentation for additional knowledge and insights. Finally, this is by no means the first time that an attempt has been made to take hold of the past so as to improve the future. Many contemporary analysts have gone all the way to Ancient Greece to grapple with modern issues. The analysis offered in this chapter differs from these contemporary analyses in three important respects: it seeks to give a stronger foundation to, and not displace or reject, modernity; it makes available knowledge of past efforts to citizens in the form of a usable past so that that rich historical experience can serve to lend support to their contemporary efforts and stimulate them to act; and it draws on the contemporary theory and practice of civic studies to show what is missing in the historical experience.

COLLECTIVE ACTION AND CONSTITUTIONAL CHOICE

Considerable progress has been made in the theoretical and practical knowledge of collective action and constitutional political economy since the pioneering work of Mancur Olson, James M. Buchanan, and Gordon Tullock in the 1960s. The lecture Elinor Ostrom delivered in Stockholm in 2009, when she received the Nobel Prize in Economic Sciences, describes the progress made in understanding the conditions under which we can expect people to engage in joint efforts.[2] This evolution directs attention to how citizens learn to become competent artisans in the creation of collective undertakings, and how observers learn to recognize that ordinary people can construct their own realities and fashion rules and norms that apply to the constitution of self-governing entities. Vincent Ostrom put it this way: "the focus of our concern is on *people* and the way they choose to relate to one another rather than on *states* or *governments* as such."[3]

A chief lesson that can be taken from these developments is that agents of constitutional choice are not confined to rulers, governments, or constituent assemblies but extend to individuals acting in a collective capacity to secure future goods. In chapter 4, Paul Dragos Aligica places in sharp relief the Bloomington scholars' recognition of the pivotal role of citizenship and civic competence as core themes of politics and political theory. The literature on common-pool resources suggests that, though self-enforcement is extraordinarily difficult, individuals who constitute their own systems and interact repeatedly with one another can, and do, self-enforce constitutions and use scarce resources in common without the degradation of the environment symbolized by the expression "the tragedy of the commons," which was popularized by Garrett Hardin's challenging article in *Science*.[4] Elinor Ostrom and her colleagues have found that "a group of principals can organize themselves voluntarily to retain the residuals of their own efforts."[5] To paraphrase Hobbes, covenants can be without a sword, just as self-governance may also be self-enforcing.[6] Equally important is the recognition that various forms of collective action can, and do, take place simultaneously and for different reasons at the micro-level and macro-level of society. Recognition that we live in a multi-constitutional world helped lead Vincent Ostrom to develop what remains his single most important legacy, the core concept of polycentricity.[7] In 1961, he introduced the term in a classic article "The Organization of Government in Metropolitan Areas: A Theoretical Inquiry," coauthored with Charles Tiebout and Robert Warren:

> "Polycentricity" connotes many centers of decision-making which are formally independent of each other…. To the extent that they take each other into account in competitive relationships, enter into various contractual and cooperative undertakings or have recourse to central mechanisms to resolve conflict, the various political jurisdictions in a metropolitan area may function in a coherent manner with consistent and predictable patterns of interacting behavior.

Subsequently, the Ostroms worked to develop a framework of analysis for tracing the different configurations of rules that apply to multiple levels and diverse types of organizations drawn from the public, private, and community-based voluntary sectors. The result is an appreciation of the overlapping realms of responsibility and functional capacities of local undertakings and the centrality of citizens as co-creators of the world in which they live. In addressing the crisis of centralized American public administration, Vincent Ostrom put it this way: "becoming aware that human beings can draw upon different conceptions and systems of ideas to fashion different social realities is a fundamental step to becoming a master artisan in public administration and in the study of human societies."[8] The emphasis is on revealing a science of citizenship at work. In creating relevant knowledge about self-governance, the Ostroms succeeded in doing two things at the same time: recognizing the existence of human agency and creative capacity and promoting those qualities and skills among human beings, whether they live in Los Angeles County, the Chicago neighborhoods, the slums of São Paulo, the mountains of Nepal, or the forests of the Amazon. Their work challenged researchers to stretch their vistas beyond the making of national constitutions in order to discover ordinary people as agents of constitutional choice creating various forms of institutions for collective action across different linguistic usages and to appreciate how those individuals can create for themselves different configurations of rules to shape and give meaning to future human interaction. From this perspective, theories of collective action and constitutional choice can help us understand how a public science of civics can emerge from the practice of self-governance. The recent work of Paul Dragos Aligica and Vlad Tarko shows that the polycentric conceptual framework is not only a robust analytical structure for the study of complex social phenomena, but also a challenging method of drawing non–ad hoc analogies between different types of self-organizing complex social systems.[9]

A CIVILIZATION OF CIVICS

As early as the 1960s, Vincent Ostrom made explicit what was often implicit in future explorations in public choice: citizens themselves must have knowledge of the principles of self-governance, the art and science of association, if they are to take part in a democracy. It was thus natural for him to turn to classic works that highlight this experience. He seldom lost the opportunity to remind readers that he regarded Tocqueville's fifth chapter in *Democracy in America* as one of the most insightful discussions of the American public enterprise systems and of the opportunities for public entrepreneurship afforded by the American political system. At the same time, like Tocqueville, he reiterated the universality of the community in order to make the point about the need to discover the extent to which the structure of basic institutions has been the primary instrument for advancing human welfare or has been the essential source of adversity among people; for though town society "has existed ever since there have been men, town liberty is something rare and fragile."[10] This led Ostrom (pers. comm.) to consider "methodological communalism" as a necessary complement to methodological individualism. For him, methodological individualism can be understood as calling on one's resources as a human being in order to gain an understanding of the incentives and aversions that are characteristic of other human beings; methodological communalism is a way of enabling us to understand what others do and accomplish as a function of living their lives in association with others. It becomes all the more important, then, to know how people draw on the exigencies experienced in everyday life and in the intergenerational lifecycle of family and kin relationships in order to establish and maintain complex and, often, long-enduring patterns of association.

The idea that people holding their destiny in their own hands begins at the local level can and does "travel" well beyond the political experience of Europe and North America, to the point that it may be possible to speak of "a civilization of civics"—that is, a universal aspiration, a way of thinking, for people to have a hand in creating forms of human interaction that promote and give meaning to civic ideals, local institutions in the constitution of democracies, and, more generally, human flourishing. Civic thinkers in the nineteenth century—from Carlo Cattaneo and Tocqueville to François Guizot and John Stuart Mill—seldom forgot that the very idea of civilization derives from *cives*, citizens as co-creators of the world in which they live. A concern for how people since times immemorial have managed to apply principles of governance to common pool resources—from pasture to water—has brought together people working on the same topic from many disciplines, organized as the International Association for the Study of Common Property. This conceptual generality made *Governing the Commons: The Evolution of Institutions for Collective Action* such an exciting and widely recognized work.[11]

A flourishing stream of scholarship on world history has found self-organizing and self-governing practices in the history of macro-political orders associated with lordship and bureaucratic autocracies of the past. There are now many scholarly studies that detail how populations of cities like Naples constructed their identity and a citizen culture in the face of Spanish domination in the sixteenth and seventeenth centuries.[12] The historical record in Asia and Africa shows that "most people in the world can call on some local tradition on which to build a modern democracy."[13] More recently, James Scott has shown that indigenous people in Upland Southeast Asia, in their desire for freedom from oppression, engaged in various sustained undertakings to successfully escape from state authority.[14] A chief problem with much of the literature on world history, including Scott's work, is its lack of attention to mechanisms that would allow indigenous peoples to engage in gains by trade over extended periods and thus advance material production as well as wealth creation. The work of the late S. R. Epstein opened an exciting avenue of research on mechanisms of self-governance and growth in premodern times,[15] but much remains to be done. In short, while exploring how people across different time periods and linguistic communities have come to share the civilization of civics, we need to pay more attention to the mechanisms of self-governance for development and modernity at the same time. History offers a rich domain of the artifactual world.

THE ARTIFACTUAL WORLD IN HISTORY
To develop a framework for analyzing the vast and diverse domain of the artifactual world in history is in itself an exercise in theory development and empirical research. The method I have adopted is that followed by Tocqueville in

dissecting the old regime in France. He approached the task "with a view to eliciting the laws of life" and "to supply a picture that while scientifically accurate may also be instructive."[16] He did not discount the gross inequalities of conditions and the political and economic hierarchies, but whenever he found, beneath the power of fixed social orders and monarchical administration, a spirit of healthy independence and human creativity he threw them in sharp relief. Following this method, it is possible to identify common features and principles of organization that help take hold of the diverse forms of human creativity and self-governance over a vast arc of time. Let me briefly describe these features.

INDIVIDUALS AS ARTISANS OF THE COMMON LIFE

There is ample historical evidence in support of the view that, since the eleventh century, ordinary people have often acted as artisans of many forms of organized existence, including spontaneous orders like exchange, markets, and related institutions such as the office of public notary (an enforcement mechanism without the Hobbesian sword).[17] The focus is not only on mere citizenship as a form of membership in the community—important as that was—but also on a distinctive set of practices involving creative agency and a commitment to joint civic ventures. The challenge of the historical record concerns whether it is possible to find robust measures in order to identify how and why expressions of citizen competence emerged and the conceptual and computational logic that led people to particular forms of social order and self-governance.

This challenge can be partially met by the knowledge coming from successive generations of chroniclers who, in their own times, treated individuals as the basic constituents of the world (malleable by others but who can shape themselves) and were equally concerned with individual competence and responsibility and team work. But the fact remains that we will probably never know what went on in the organization of most local collective undertakings. It is difficult to reconstruct in each instance who initiated such collective ventures, how many participants were actually involved, and what information they actually had about their own situations. Still, the wealth of empirical evidence generated by different historians from different parts of Europe is robust enough to remove shadows and false light, and to reveal that people from Flanders to Sicily and from Castile to Germany acted collectively to obtain or establish local collective efforts, charters, and the like.

There is ample historical evidence in support of the view that, since the eleventh century, ordinary people have often acted as artisans of many forms of organized existence, including spontaneous orders like exchange, markets, and related institutions such as the office of public notary

The wealth of empirical evidence points to multiple facts. First "the quite prolific statutes of medieval towns are an inexhaustible reservoir for assessing the virile strength of populist forms of government."[18] Second, stimulated by the growth of the profession of public notary and the legal profession—to the point that civil litigation appeared to be a favored pastime among different strata of society as early as the ninth century—this rich record extends to almost all other aspects of organized activity, including dispute settlements, charters, and chronicles of all sorts. Finally, local statutes, chronicles, and other such records were often produced on paper made to last and carefully kept as documentary proofs by public notaries. This helps explain why contestations between nobles and villagers often took the form of what Caroline Castiglione in her research on seventeenth century Latium has called "adversarial literacy."[19] The archival research of Gérard Delille on local and central authorities in the Western Mediterranean between the fifteenth and the eighteenth centuries has lent support to, broadened, and extended our understanding of two important facts: first, ordinary people in pre-modern times were far from being hapless victims of circumstances, and, second, the challenges they faced in meeting multiple threats posed by factions to local collective efforts.

THE MULTIFORM NATURE OF CREATIVE ARTISANSHIP

In *Law and Revolution,* Harold J. Berman indicated that the basic principles of multi-constitutional governance were worked out in the free cities of Germany and Italy long before the Americans confronted the problems of constitutional choice.[20] The basic principles involved are the following: (a) covenanting with one another that also extended to neighborhood associations, guilds, and many types of business and trade ventures (*lex mercatoria*); (b) the rejection of hereditary rule as the sole way for leaders to emerge (*principatus perpetuus*); (c) the affirmation of government officials appointed for limited, secular terms of office (*principatus ad tempus*); and (d) the rule of law.

By the thirteenth century, the practice of self-organization and self-governance, including relations based on contractual relations, extended to almost all forms of known collective activity and undertaking throughout Western Europe. Each collective undertaking was organized as a *universitas*, and what distinguished one *universitas* from another was the task(s) each set for itself, with the result that almost every town (or village, as the study of English villagers in the thirteenth century by George Homans suggested long ago[21]) had its own multi-constitutional world, albeit organized by male family heads. Each collective undertaking had its own jurisdiction (*jurisdictio*), authority (*gubernaculum*), and the power to regulate itself (*praeceptio*) through a variety of means. Size was not a factor as such, for each entity, small or large, possessed a constitutional freedom (if only in the form of privilege and not "right" in the modern meaning of that term), jurisdiction, and internal regulations.

From England to Sicily, multiple political orders and horizontal and vertical bonds emerged to exist simultaneously and sequentially on the same plane. Much of the work by Susan Reynolds on kingdoms and communities in Western Europe between 900 and 1300 is to redress "the tendency to undervalue the horizontal bonds in medieval society" without anachronistically idealizing them.[22] The "communal movement" of the twelfth century did not introduce new ideas and values of association. The conceptual and computational logic necessary to form a social order and governance was already there. "All the collectivities which abound in the sources of the twelfth and thirteenth centuries drew their cohesion from ideas and values which were already deep-rooted."[23] For example, Sicilian cities were vibrant with life as "sites of Roman law courts, municipal night-watch companies, armies of harbor officials, schools, tariff codes, almshouses and hospitals, more tax collectors, taverns, warehouses and urban magistrates endlessly copying, invoking, exercising, and seeking to expand their cities' cherished and obsessively guarded *consuetudines*. Each community followed its own customs but remained opened to outside contact."[24]

Thus, the local multi-constitutional world included considerable diversity in organizational form and scope with common underlying principles of various forms of self and joint rule. These undertakings covered almost all aspects of organized existence: work; life goods that had public and private characteristics, like food and health; and common-pool resources ranging from woodland to churches and neighborhoods. In varying degrees, it was possible to find in almost any community a public space (*res publica*) that permitted problem solving through the spontaneous creation of joint undertakings of all sorts. One of the best examples of this comes from fifteenth-century Florence. Probably the greatest architectural puzzle of that period was how to construct the dome of the Santa Maria del Fiore Cathedral, which still stands today. The puzzle was successfully resolved through open competition for the design of the dome, and through a variety of joint undertakings involving teamwork of all sorts and several monitoring and accountability mechanisms. Mechanisms of exchange included long-distance trade. Historians are slowly bringing to light the role of women as business entrepreneurs in several trade ventures between Venice and Constantinople over several centuries, and probably the same applies to other trading centers from Lubeck to Messina. The port cities of Alexandria, Beirut, and Smyrna played similar roles in the Levant.

Presumptive knowledge is a chief problem in historical explorations. When a practice (good or bad) is found operating at any one point in time, one of two things happens: either it is assumed by implication that the practice lasts forever, or there is a tendency to project back that practice (or failings found in the nineteenth century) without bothering to investigate subsequent periods. As a result, there has been a tendency to paint either a positive or a negative picture and to ignore the capacity of people in history to affect or make improvements. When the problem of presumptive knowledge is duly taken into account, other issues emerge.

Against the historical backdrop sketched here, contemporary concerns about the need of civic education for future generations of citizens become even more compelling.[25] To paraphrase Elinor Ostrom, the key sets of ideas that modern citizens must understand in order to sustain the world of civics were, in the past, regularly passed on to young people as they participated in a wide array of community activities in which neighbors helped neighbors and the value of being trustworthy and extending reciprocity were taught by example. Young people equally understood the multiple threats that existed to any group of people wishing to accomplish a joint objective as well as the ways to avoid the tragedy of the commons and to prevent threats from escalating. They encountered such exigencies of everyday life at home and in their neighborhoods. It is doubtful that young people encounter them today, when they are taught that all they have to do is to vote in every election. A chief problem that plagued the rich tapestry of local undertakings sketched here is the lack of overlapping jurisdictions—or what Cattaneo called "the federal idea"[26] and Vincent Ostrom called polycentricity. The federal idea, or polycentricity, and the ways to make it operational were not available before the seventeenth century. The creation of national monarchies did not help this discovery either.

CONTINUITIES AND RUPTURES

In *The Old Regime and the French Revolution,* Tocqueville succinctly highlighted continuity and ruptures: "Transported overseas from feudal Europe and free to develop in total independence, the rural parish of the Middle Ages became the township of New England. Emancipated from their seigneur, but controlled at every turn by an all-powerful government, it took in France ... the form of paternal government."[27] Much of the literature on long-term political and economic changes in Europe is, unfortunately, not helpful in understanding this continuity and rupture because of the tendency to view "state capture" as unproblematic.

Political transformations. The creation of national monarchies did not, as a rule, work in favor of institutions of local self-governance. What kind of civic engagement could flourish in national political systems characterized by a high degree of centralized government and administration is still an open empirical question, made all the more difficult to answer by the tendency of much of social science to view unitary systems as unproblematic and by the centralizing tendencies of supranational organizations like the European Union. This is why the message conveyed by Václav Havel about "the power of the powerless" continues to have resonance for citizens and social scientists alike.[28] Still, it was possible to find under the power of national monarchies—as Tocqueville did in the case of the regional assembly of Languedoc in France—vestiges of local and regional independence and local laws and privileges that kept alive a certain sense of local independence and problem solving. The puzzle of mixed government that had eluded Aquinas, Dante, and Marsilius of Padua was resolved by Althusius. In his work, the sovereignty of the people operating at the grassroots level could now coexist with the effective authority of the ruler. But Althusius did more than theorize. He actually described the Dutch practice, following the defeat of Spanish rule.

Economic transformations. With the Enlightenment, the centrality of exchange, commerce, and entrepreneurship emerged as a liberating mechanism in full force, under the rubric of public, or civil, economy. The emphasis on "public" or "civil" rather than "statist" political economy served to affirm the centrality of individuals as artisans and practitioners of spontaneous orders. Montesquieu and Adam Smith pointed to the growth of cities, while more recent scholarship is discovering the interconnection of ideas that brought together Naples and Scotland in the Enlightenment in order to sketch sophisticated blends of institutional interaction between public and private institutions.[29] This mixture went beyond the narrow confines of "state and market" to give meaning to trade as *socialitas,* or reciprocal assistance, and to convey a strong positive relationship between trade and public trust and happiness. It is on this understanding of public economy that the modern public science of civics can build.

CONCLUSION

The sovereignty of national states and their expanding reach in policy areas have tended to eclipse the importance of cultivating self-governing citizens as artisans of the common life. This chapter has sought to retrieve the earlier practices of self-governance for what it can tell us about that tradition. Clearly, the public science of civics as an inter-civilizational practice of self-governance needs further elaboration. For this reason, the preceding analysis has truly been a preliminary exploration, a work in progress. However, one thing should be clear enough: bringing theory to practice is not just a preoccupation confined to Tocquevillian analysts. Rather, it is a universal preoccupation concerned with the art and science of cultivating self-governing citizens. Current efforts to bring theory to practice in civic studies can build on a rich heritage.

NOTES

1. The preparation of this chapter draws on research supported by the Social Science and Humanities Research Council of Canada (SSHRC 410-2011-0698), help which I wish to acknowledge.
2. Elinor Ostrom, "Beyond Markets and States: Polycentric Governance of Complex Economic Systems," *American Economic Review* 100 (June 2010): 641–72.
3. Vincent Ostrom, "The Centrality of Local Institutions in the Constitution of Democracies," in *The Quest to Understand Human Affairs: Natural Resource Policy and Essays on Community and Collective Choice,* ed. Barbara Allen, vol. 1 (Lanham, MD: Lexington, 2011), 341.
4. Hardin, "The Tragedy of the Commons," *Science* 162 (1968): 1243–8.
5. Elinor Ostrom, *Governing the Commons: The Evolution of Institutions for Collective Action,* (New York: Cambridge University Press, 1990), 250; see also Marco Casari and C. R. Plott, "Decentralized Management of Common Property Resources: Experiment with a Centuries-Old Institution," *Journal of Economic Behavior & Organization* 51, no. 2 (2003): 217–47.
6. Elinor Ostrom, J. Walker, and R. Gardner, "Covenants with and without a Sword: Self-Governance Is Possible," *American Political Science Review* 86, no. 2 (1992): 404–17.
7. Michael McGinnis and Elinor Ostrom, "Reflections on Vincent Ostrom, Public Administration, and Polycentricity," *Public Administration Review* 20, no.1 (2011): 15–25.
8. Vincent Ostrom, *The Intellectual Crisis in American Public Administration* (Tuscaloosa, AL: University of Alabama Press, 2008), xxix.
9. Paul Dragos Aligica and Vlad Tarko, "Polycentricity: From Polanyi to Ostrom, and Beyond," *Governance: An International Journal of Policy, Administration and Institutions* 25, no. 2 (April 2012): 237–62.
10. Tocqueville, *Democracy in America* (Indianapolis: Liberty Fund, 2010), 101.
11. Elinor Ostrom, *Governing the Commons: The Evolution of Institutions for Collective Action* (New York: Cambridge University Press, 1990).
12. For an excellent introduction, see John Marino, *Becoming Neapolitan: Citizen Culture in Baroque Naples* (Baltimore: Johns Hopkins University Press, 2011).
13. S. Mulhberger and P. Paine, "Democracy's Place in World History," *Journal of World History* 4, no. 1 (1993): 26.
14. Scott, *The Art of Not Being Governed: An Anarchist History of Upland Southeast Asia* (New Haven, CT: Yale University Press, 2009).
15. Epstein, *An Island for Itself: Economic Development and Social Change in Late Medieval Sicily* (New York: Cambridge University Press, 1992); *Freedom and Growth: The Rise of States and*

Markets in Europe, 1300–1750 (New York: Routledge, 2000). See also Regina Grafe, *Distant Tyrrany: Markets, Power, and Backwardness in Spain 1650–1800* (Princeton: Princeton University Press, 2012); and Helen Nader, *Liberty in Absolutist Spain: The Habsburg Sale of Towns, 1516– 1700* (Baltimore: The Johns Hopkins University Press, 1990).

16. Tocqueville, *The Old Regime and the French Revolution* (Garden City, NY: Doubleday Anchor Books, 1956), xii.

17. A good introduction to this topic is Laurie Nussdorfer, *Brokers of Public Trust: Notaries in Early Modern Rome* (Baltimore: The Johns Hopkins University Press, 2009).

18. Walter Ullmann, *Principles of Government and Politics in the Middle Ages* (London: Methuen, 1978), 219.

19. Castiglione, *Patrons and Adversaries: Nobles and Villagers in Italian Politics 1640–1760* (New York: Oxford University Press, 2005).

20. Berman, *Law and Revolution: The Formation of the Western Legal Tradition* (Cambridge, MA: Harvard University Press, 1983).

21. Homans, *English Villagers of the Thirteenth Century* (New York: Russell and Russell, 1960).

22. Reynolds, *Kingdoms and Communities in Western Europe, 900–1300* (Oxford: Clarendon Press, 1984), 1.

23. Ibid.

24. C. R. Backman, *The Decline and Fall of Medieval Sicily: Politics, Religion and Economy in the Reign of Frederick III, 1296–1337* (New York: Cambridge University Press, 1995), 20.

25. Peter Levine, *The Future of Democracy. Developing the Next Generation of American Citizens* (Medford, MA: Tufts University Press, 2007; and Elinor Ostrom, "The Need for Civic Education. A Collective Action Perspective." Paper (Bloomington, IN: Workshop in Political Theory and Policy Analysis, Indiana University, 1998).

26. Filippo Sabetti, *Self-Government and Civilization: The Political Thought of Carlo Cattaneo* (Lanham: Lexington Books, 2010).

27. Tocqueville, *The Old Regime,* 48, 51.

28. Vaclav Havel, *The Power of the Powerless* (Armonk, NY: M. E. Sharpe, 1985).

29. John Robertson, *The Case for the Enlightenment: Scotland and Naples, 1680–1760* (New York: Cambridge University Press, 2005). See also Filippo Sabetti, "Public Happiness as the Wealth of Nations: The Rise of Political Economy in Naples in a Comparative Perspective," *California Italian Studies* 3, no. 1 (2012): 1–31.

Citizenship, Political Competence, and Civic Studies: The Ostromian Perspective

Paul Dragos Aligica

4

THE WORK OF Vincent Ostrom and Elinor Ostrom is multifaceted and inter-disciplinary, but its most lasting impact comes from the fact that it has advanced a profound theoretical vision about governance and governance-related processes. Among the contributions for which this work has become famous and influential are the political economy approach to the analysis of non-market decision settings, the development of the concept of polycentricity as an analytic and interpretive framework, the emphasis on coproduction as a key element in public policy strategies and processes, and the construction of the institutional analysis and development framework as a methodological tool for social and policy sciences. These and other related themes are indeed a trademark of the research program they created, and, as such, deserve to be well recognized.

Yet, there is one crucial element of their work that has been less recognized and discussed, despite its importance. Their vision of governance and normative political economy is strongly anchored in a well-articulated theory of civic competence and a well-defined view of citizenship and civic behavior. Very few have noticed that once the themes of political competence and citizenship get introduced into the picture, the perspective on the Ostroms' work gains instantly an entirely new dimension. It is, hence, a great loss that their contribution to civic studies—seen both as a conceptual reflection and an input to governance processes—is less discussed, although it occupies, in the end, such an essential position in their system. This chapter will be an attempt to focus on this issue. The chapter will start with the more visible and relatively better known views of the Ostroms regarding citizenship and civic and political competence. Then it will focus on the less known and less understood dimension that pertains to a deeper and more profound level of their perspective: a possibilist epistemology and ontology of social order and change in which citizenship (and civic studies) plays a decisive role. In combination, the two parts will show why the Ostroms' interest in civic studies should not be seen as a mere footnote or marginal extension of their main work, but rather as part and parcel of their core message.

SOCIAL SCIENCES, SELF-GOVERNANCE, CITIZENSHIP,
AND THE "ART AND SCIENCE OF ASSOCIATION"

In an academic environment in which the mainstream was fascinated with a vision
of "positive science" and obsessed with the purity of "scientific method," the
Ostroms were never shy to acknowledge (and even boast) that their social scientific
work was about the practical intricacies of human governance and, more precisely,
about the ways free individuals may be able to better self-govern themselves.
They put at the core of their research program an explicitly assumed, normative
(political and philosophical) stance: self-governance. Governments should not
"exercise tutelage over Societies and steer and direct those Societies." But if
"people are to rule," then "members of society should know how to govern
themselves."[1] The Ostroms' work is avowedly meant to contribute to the creation
of a collective cumulative knowledge base that is to be applied by citizens to
governance processes. In fact, they saw their efforts as part of "the central tradition
of human and social studies:

> There is no better testimony for that than the questions that structure our work:
> How can fallible human beings achieve and sustain self-governing entities and
> self-governing ways of life? How can individuals influence the rules that
> structure their lives? Similar questions were asked by Aristotle and other
> foundational social and political philosophers. These were the concerns of
> Madison, Hamilton and de Tocqueville."[2]

In other words, the Ostroms strove to contribute from a contemporary perspective
(i.e., using the intellectual tools of the age and the historical insights gained so far)
to a long tradition of creating relevant knowledge about self-governance,
knowledge to be used by individuals organizing and reorganizing their coexistence in human societies. This may also be seen as something having to do with
long-term social evolution, a collective cultural and social phenomenon, having
at its center knowledge passed from one generation to another—augmented by
some generations, diminished by others, restored by others. This is not knowledge for knowledge's sake or for reasons having to do with the institutional
stringencies of careers in academic settings, but rather it is knowledge for improving
our ability to organize for self-governance as citizens:

> [O]ne of our greatest priorities at the Workshop has been to ensure that our
> research contributes to the education of future citizens, entrepreneurs in the
> public and private spheres, and officials at all levels of government. We have
> a distinct obligation to participate in this educational process as well as to
> engage in the research enterprise so that we build a cumulative knowledge
> base that may be used to sustain democratic life. Self-governing, democratic
> systems are always fragile enterprises. Future citizens need to understand
> that they participate in the constitution and reconstitution of rule-governed
> polities. And they need to learn the 'art and science of association.' If we fail
> in this, all our investigations and theoretical efforts are useless.[3]

This position leads to a double criticism of what was seen as the mainstream
conventional wisdom on democracy. First is a criticism of the incomplete understanding of the institutional nature of democracy. Second is a criticism of a
limited understanding of the role of citizenship and political competence in a

democratic system. The Bloomington institutionalists part ways with their fellow Public Choice scholars. The latter seem to believe that the scientific study of (and accumulation of data about) the workings of the institutions of democracy, and especially elections and bureaucracies, has to be a sufficient knowledge and ideational basis for the operation and improvement of the governance of a social system.

But, for the Ostroms, the excessive concentration on the formal and standard apparatus of democracy was an error. Vincent Ostrom was very vocal in this respect: "'One person, one vote, majority rule' is an inadequate and superficial formulation for constituting viable democratic societies."[4] Popular elections are necessary but not sufficient. There are, he asserted, "more fundamental conditions" than that for creating and governing viable democratic societies.[5] In fact, elections, political parties, and governing coalitions can lead to social strife, chaos, and institutional collapse.

> What it means to live in a democratic society is much more demanding than electing representatives who form governments. Not only are democratic societies constructed around the essential place of citizens in those societies, but they cannot be maintained without the knowledge, moral integrity, skill, and intelligibility of citizens in the cultivation of those societies. Calling all persons in all States "citizens" and all States "republics" is a misleading use of language and an erroneous way of conceptualizing political "realities."[6]

The illusion created by the view of social science according to which the specific attitudes and belief systems of the social actors are ultimately of marginal relevance for governance and institutional design has created the conditions for a paradoxical situation. Entire corpuses of institutional theory and political science are built on the principles of methodological individualism. But then, in the next breath, they decline to consider of interest the individuals' patterns of beliefs, competencies, and attitudes. Yet, it is uncontroversial that some sets of beliefs and attitudes make for good governance, and some don't. "Citizenship" matters. In an era of scientism, we tend to forget that many institutional pathologies of modern governance may in fact be the results of "the superficial way we think about citizenship in democratic societies."[7]

The future of human civilization, writes Vincent Ostrom, "will not just happen"; it "will be constructed and will require attentive care."[8] As Filippo Sabetti synthesizes it in chapter 3, in Vincent Ostrom's methodological individualism, "individuals are seen as artisans of the common life." A focus on citizenship is a focus on a world of possibilities, on the "computational" and "combinatorial" logics of alternative decision paths and alternative institutional constructions. If we agree that the political order of the future is constructed on an ongoing basis, then the problem is in what measure is constructed by accident and force and in what measure is constructed by reflection and choice. Something called "citizenship," or "political and civic competence," should matter. Self-governance based on reflection and choice is coextensive with the notion of constructive participation of citizens in the creation and maintenance of social order. In these circumstances, the very idea of a "science of citizenship in democratic systems of order" should be something expected and normal.

Those concerned with the constitution of democratic societies are required to give critical attention to the development of a science of citizenship and civic enlightenment. The idea of self-governance draws attention to the notion of constructive participation of citizens in social order. That science should not be confined to the education of students in schools. It should be a science of association that is studied and applied by all as we assume responsibility for living our lives and learning how to work with others under variable and changing conditions that reach out to global proportions.[9]

These are, in a nutshell, the elements constituting the better-known face of the (otherwise not much recognized and understood) Ostromian position on civic competence, citizenship, and civic studies. All of the above are intrinsically related, being facets of a same position that are connected logically in a coherent viewpoint. We are not talking here about a mere footnote or a marginal extension of the Ostroms' better-known empirical and theoretical work in political economy and institutional theory. We are talking about something at the core of their project and their system of thought. Citizenship is both the fuel and the pivot of a free and democratic social order. Being aware of this, and understanding its nature and its ongoing transformation and adjustment in correlation with the evolution of its operating environment, is an important task. In brief, the Ostroms articulated a consistent vision in which the problems of governance and institutional theory of democratic social order cannot be viewed in separation from the problems of citizenship, civic competence, and civic studies. Even if their contribution were limited to that, their place in the genealogy of civic studies would be assured. However, there is more in the Ostromian position. A closer look at their writings—especially Vincent Ostrom's—reveals the existence of an additional dimension that is less visible and even less familiar, that pertains to a deeper and more profound level.

CIVIC COMPETENCE, CITIZENSHIP AND THE COUNTERVAILING POWERS PRINCIPLE
A closer reading of Vincent Ostrom's discussion of the philosophical principles of self-governance reveals that the Bloomington scholars' recognition of the pivotal role of citizenship and civic competence is ultimately part of a rather sophisticated understanding of a core theme of politics and political theory. Ostrom joins an entire lineage of eminent political thinkers that consider the issue of governance as ultimately a problem of control of power through its separation and checks-and-balances arrangements. He is thus part of the tradition that, from Polybius to the Federalists via Contarini and Montesquieu, recognizes the control, not the employment, of power as the primary problem of politics and subscribes to the doctrine of separation or division of power—a tradition that, as Sabetti notes in chapter 4—is also related to the "mixed government" doctrine. "I cannot imagine how democratic societies can be sustained without checks and balances in systems of dispersed authority," Ostrom wrote, adding that "using power to check power is essential to lawful republics."[10] His place in this illustrious tradition is close to that of Madison, who in his interpretation "proposed that a principle of opposite and rival interests could apply to the constitution of order through the whole system of human

affairs," which includes "the supreme powers of the State" but obviously is not limited to it."[11]

That being said, Vincent Ostrom's take on the operation of the principle has a special twist. In his assessment, the mechanics of mere, brute counterbalance between the centers of power is not sufficient. Neither is it sufficient to have an overarching set of rules regulating their interactions as a second-order device. The ultimate key, essential for the system's functioning, is the way social actors behave—or, more precisely, their attitudes and strategies within the field of power forces at specific critical junctures. We thus get back to citizenship and civic competence.

Behind the checks-and-balances principle, Ostrom identifies a huge problem: conflict and its escalation. A system based on countervailing powers has built into it, by design, tension and conflict. Conflict is unavoidable. The problem is not its elimination (which is impossible) but how it is contained and managed. We need to acknowledge that, in some cases, the spontaneous and quasi-mechanical reciprocal checks-and-balances system is not going to work. Escalation may take place. It is the very nature of escalation that it may take off and amplify from minor tensions. The threat of escalation is real and deadly for social order.

In such circumstances, elaborates Ostrom, there are two scenarios. In the first, citizens are "ignorant of the principles of self-governance"; they lack the political capabilities to manage the challenge. In this scenario, we "would expect the use of power to check power through opposite and rival interests to yield stalemate and then to escalate to a point where the various opposite and rival interests in a society were at war with one another." A different outcome is expected in the second scenario, "when people come to expect that conflicts require recourse to processes of conflict resolution." In this case, "conflict situations become the basis for inquiry about the sources of conflict and how conflict situations have the possibility of being transformed."[12] To be more precise, one may imagine two types of solutions to the problem of escalation. The first is summarized by the notion of threats and counter-threats out of which mutually assured destruction is one extreme variant. The idea is that a reciprocal threat system leads to various forms of equilibrium. The second type of solution is different. It takes as a starting point the threats to the system, but adds to it a process of mutual adjustment via communication and negotiation that is set up by institutional procedures. It is obvious that this second type of solution pushes the discussion beyond the realm of mere power politics and institutional incentives and their governing rules. Something additional seems to be needed in order to cope with the intrinsic problem of conflict and escalation via this type of approach—an attitude, a know-how, a knowledge base, a culture. We are thus again back to the very idea of political competence, citizenship, and civics. Social actors need to be mentally and attitudinally equipped in ways that enable them to avoid escalation and, via a flexible and informed use of institutional procedures, to manage the conflict intrinsic to the system. This attitudinal and mental competence is the foundation on which citizenship is based.

Despite his reputation as a rational choice institutionalist, Vincent Ostrom was insistent that the system of institutionalized countervailing powers he advocated as being essential to the constitution of order "can only work with the development of a culture of inquiry in which conflict can be addressed in a problem-solving mode of inquiry rather than in a way that provokes fight-sets where threats and counter-threats easily escalate into violent confrontations."[13] Ostrom refered frequently to Montesquieu's view that using power to check power depends on "the virtues of moral communities that seek to use the opportunities associated with conflict as a means of achieving conflict resolution."[14] Successful governance depends on the awareness of this basic reality and on social actors' capability to act on that awareness—i.e., to make it operational. The presence of such mental and attitudinal profiles and capabilities in a society, and the ensuing science and art of association to be practiced by them, do not in any way guarantee success. However, "possibilities of failure can be reduced."

The argument thus places in a clear light both the idea of "civic studies" and the relevance of the type of knowledge it represents. There is one important thing that should be noted in this respect: the emphasis put on "inquiry," on the idea of a "culture of *inquiry*," on people understanding "the utility of forms and procedures in constructing a due process of inquiry bounded by a due process of law."[15] That "inquiry" is considered such an important feature tells us two things: first, citizenship could not be associated with mere routines, norms, and rule-guided behavior; second, citizenship means active, systematic investigation, analysis, and evaluation. Citizenship is something that requires both discipline and learning processes. The institutional artifacts related to the checks-and-balances system and, even more, the nature of its additional supportive elements, Vincent Ostrom noted, do not come naturally, and their role and functioning are not understood spontaneously and naturally by most people. Many things, both in the institutional architecture and the accommodating and facilitating attitudes and ideas needed to successfully master the task, are not intuitive and commonsensical. They need clarification, analysis, articulation. They need to be explained and disseminated:

> Human institutions are, unfortunately, subject to counterintuitive relationships that pose a serious challenge to common sense in a democratic society. If common sense were sufficient to cope with problems in this world, we might expect people intuitively to understand what would be required in coping with any situation. Our common-sense intuitions are clearly unsatisfactory, and we must go to substantial effort to establish counterintuitive relationships that occur in many problematical situations.[16]

Hence, the need of addressing the challenge in a "problem-solving mode of inquiry." Note that, in the end, the label does not matter. We could, for example, use the notion of "civic studies" to designate this substantive effort in clarification. But, irrespective of the label used, the idea and reality of "civic studies" come to the fore on two levels. First, they come together as an ingredient in the functioning of institutional arrangements—a key component in the cultural and process knowledge mix that supports the dynamic adjustment of governance systems. Secondly, they perform a reflexivity function at a meta-level. The human mind could turn on and reflect on the artifacts, such as institutional and governance arrangements, and on itself, as designer of those artifacts. Thus, "civic studies" represents an expression of a particular feature of human systems: social reflexivity, the ability of a system to contemplate and study itself and then to transfer the insights thus gained as a renewed input in the real-life process. And thus, one can see here the reemerging contours of the idea of civic studies and civic culture, citizenship or political competence, as part of a larger, adaptive, social learning, collective knowledge process.

That being said, there is an additional element in Vincent Ostrom's argument that deserves a special note. The quote above is rather telling. It is tempting to think about civic competence and civic studies as possessing the commonsensical plain characteristics of any human instrumentality. But Ostrom warned us that there is something in civics and civics-related inquiries that touches on the counterintuitive and may go against common sense and conventional wisdom. Even when one may see "civics" as a mere training doctrine or an enterprise aiming at introducing principles and evidence-based social practices, one should not forget that, sooner or later, the solutions or principles may come to clash with conventional wisdom. As such, they presuppose an effort in clarification whose stake is even greater, as it may go against popular intuitions and opinions or, even more, against centers of power and dominance.

> The significance of any science turns upon its capacity to clarify that which is counterintuitive. This problem is especially great in any system of governance that depends upon the use of power to check power by opposite and rival interests. The equilibrating tendencies in such a system of relationships may be seriously distorted if counterintuitive relationships become manifest in key linkages. Under those circumstances, equilibrating tendencies can be transformed into patterns of dominance that permit some to exploit others.[17]

To sum up, the task of preempting such dysfunctional situations by creating conceptual tools to identify and understand them, and then to diffuse the insights thus gained among the citizens, is neither trivial nor easy. To harness for governance purposes the potential of the system of separation of powers and of checks and balances, and to deal with the conflict and escalation it engenders as well as the counterintuitive situations it may induce in "key linkages," requires a disciplined, systematic way of understanding and analyzing the principles and processes at work in such systems. Specific ideas, beliefs, and attitudes that permit institutional structures to contain and manage power stand at the core of humans' endeavor for self-governance. Understanding this nuance restarts "civic studies" at a deeper level.

Citizens themselves must have knowledge of the principles of self-governance

INTENTIONALITY, ARTIFACT, CIVIC COMPETENCE, CITIZENSHIP:
THE EPISTEMOLOGICAL AND ONTOLOGICAL DIMENSION

So far, we have seen how the Ostromian approach to citizenship and civics emerged from a theory of politics and institutions that is rather realist in its focus on the problem of power and its control. It is not so much about human flourishing or other maximalist "good society" goals as it is about a minimalist condition of power containment and administration as a prerequisite for any "good society." We have now a more nuanced understanding of the Bloomington scholars' position in this respect. However, the argument has yet another level that grows naturally as an extension or corollary of the positions outlined so far. Its most profound feature is that it brings to the fore the epistemological and ontological dimensions of the problem. Vincent Ostrom follows the logic of citizenship and civic competence beyond the obvious dimension of political theory. He makes explicit what otherwise would have remained hidden and implicit: the ontology and epistemology of social order seen in their relationship with the human mind and human action.

The context is straightforward. The Ostroms were never very happy with the epistemological and methodological trends generated in the social sciences by positivism. Elinor Ostrom, in the book she edited on strategies of inquiry, discussed under the title "Beyond Positivism" the situation at the beginning of the second half of the twentieth century, when fashionable positivism-inspired methods were taking the social sciences by storm. Thus, in her assessment, many graduate students lacking a proper undergraduate philosophical, logical, or quantitative training came to "take heavy courseloads in statistics and methods and fewer courses where they might be exposed to the development of systematic substantive theories":

> The combined effect of this recruitment process interacting with this type of socialization may have produced a "know nothing" era in the discipline. Many scholars who presumed they were building our new empirical foundation did indeed know very little about substance and about the relationship of the statistical languages they used to the absence of theoretical models to which the language of data analysis should have been related. The criteria for what would be accepted as "facts" became a significant correlation coefficient or a high R^2, even when it meant the acceptance of nonsense or the rejection of long-established knowledge.[18]

Vincent Ostrom, in turn, identified and criticized a view that was epistemological in nature but that has penetrated "political discourse in the twentieth century."[19] According to this view, systems of governance operate under physical law–like regularities up to the point that "the method of the natural sciences are applied to the investigation of political phenomena" without any hesitation or second thought. But that, he noted, misses something essential: the special nature of "intentionality" and its role "in construing the meaning of political experience."[20] Social order is largely artifactual and shaped by intentions. It is a construction based on the activities and ideas of social agents. This is a reality, a "fact," and as such it should make a difference for our research strategies. These research strategies need to consider the *sui generis* character of the "reality" they are dealing with. Hence the importance of intentionality and the normative and ideal benchmarks for what otherwise one may take as pure positive analysis. Relying on "brute empiricism" gives us nothing else than meaningless "facts," in the absence of intentions and normative ideals. The "facts" that we observe in human societies, Vincent Ostrom explained following John Searle, are manifestations of "institutional facts." They are "artifacts," "patterns of order" having a distinctive ontological status.[20]

If we manage to avoid "brute empiricism," Ostrom argued, and "if political experience is conceived to be artifactual (i.e., created by reference to human knowledge)," then the focus changes. The social sciences and the study of governance are not about "covering laws" or "natural regularities," but rather they are about how "intentionality and knowledgeable calculations" generate the "living realities" of the social and political realm. "The whole world in which we function as participants in communities of being, begins to take on different potentialities."[22]

In the end, this is not a mere problem of epistemology and methodology. Vincent Ostrom is bold and stubborn enough to follow the argument to its ontological conclusions, despite the unfashionable nature of the exercise. After all, social ontology was one of the last things on the "to explore" list of social scientists in the twentieth century. Ostrom was insistent that, if the artifactual character of institutions is neglected, an entire ontological realm as well as the springs that fuel it would be missed too. It is a self-reinforcing procedure: missing the ontological reality leads to methodological and epistemological problems that, in their turn, reinforce the ontological blindness. Omitting the choice and cognition aspects leads to missing the key mechanisms or processes by which the social realm and its governance are constituted. At best, they are relegated to the level of derivative or superstructural extensions of more basic forces or variables:

> The application of natural science methods to the study of political phenomena during the twentieth century has meant the abandonment of any serious preoccupation with the critical problems of [choice and cognition] that inform the artisanship inherent in the design and alteration of systems of governance as these are constituted and re-constituted. Political science in the twentieth century has become a science without an explicit understanding of the critical role of theory as a system of conceptual-computational logics that applies to the design of different systems of government.[23]

There are two major ideas underlying Ostrom's argument. Both have significant implications for the "civics" theme. The first is the idea that the "artifactual" dimension of social systems is a distinct ontological realm. It emerges from the biological realm and takes on a dynamics of its own, generating, as Filippo Sabetti puts it in chapter 4, "an artifactual world in history." In this artifactual world, intentionality and computational logics may take different forms, and social order and its complex combinations of institutional arrangements grow and evolve in specific directions as a function of that.

> The earth has been transformed into a human habitat that is a visibly different "reality" than the earth in its "natural" condition. Pierre Thielhard de Chardin characterizes this transformation as a noosphere, a sphere shaped by human knowledge which has its analogue in the biosphere, a sphere shaped by the existence of life. Artifacts cannot be understood as natural occurrences. In explaining artifactual constructions, we are required to account for human artisanship and the conceptual-computational considerations that entered into the design and creation of artifactual constructions.[24]

The second major idea is that the excessive naturalization of the social sciences leads to the abandonment of a preoccupation with the constitutive role of choice and cognition. But choice, cognition, and "combinatorial logics" are exactly the foundations of citizenship and civic competence, and they manifest with particular force and specific results in those systems that experiment with self-governance. On the one hand, it seems rather obvious that the quality and quantity of "civic competence" should make a difference in the way a governance system is both constituted and administered. On the other hand, when the ontology and epistemology of your paradigm doesn't allow you to conceptualize this properly—when, in the underlying philosophy of a social science paradigm, ideas, cognition, and individuals' collective decisions based on various computational logics do not matter—it is difficult, if possible at all, to make sense of phenomena such as civic competence and citizenship.

In conjunction, these two ideas outline the larger context, the appropriate "big picture" into which we need to place and address the problems of citizenship and civic studies, as key ingredients of constitutive arrangements dealing with the control and management of power:

> The challenge facing us in exploring the problem of "constitutional rule and shared power" is to reconsider the epistemological and metaphysical grounds on which we stand. Human beings have been agents in an extraordinary transformation of the world of nature into an artifactual realm. This artifactual realm uses the materials and processes of nature and transforms them through the use of human knowledge and artisanship to serve human purposes.[25]

That is to say, human beings and their social order are part of a great evolutionary process that is generating an entirely new realm. Within this realm created by intentionality, knowledge, and artisanship, "citizenship" and its corollary, "civic studies," are both phenomena that result from the process and factors pushing the process forward in possible new configurations. It is crucial to remember that the domain of the artifactual world of the "noosphere" is vast and diverse. In the interplay between human intentionality and cognition, on the one hand, and the environment in its evolution, on the other, there are many possible combinations, and they may generate a variety of forms of order and governance systems.

The key difference, as Vincent Ostrom explained, is the difference between, on the one side, those systems of governance that are based on citizenship aiming at self-governance and, on the other side, those systems in which "Governments exercise tutelage over Societies and steer and direct those Societies."[26] The two ideal types defining the polar model of order should be the basic lenses for assessing the nature and evolution of the realm of the artifactual. Approaching them, the logic of the analysis leads sooner or later back to the "computational logic" of the actors involved in its generation. Ultimately, such macro-level, structural, and ontological dimensions are a matter of how individuals think and act in constructing the social order surrounding them. How do they conceive governance? Do they see and think "like a state"? Or do they see and think "like a citizen"? These are the key questions.

When Tocqueville wrote *Democracy in America*, he recognized that a new conceptual-computational logic was required for the constitution of democratic societies if human beings under conditions of increasing equality were to achieve and maintain substantial freedom in their relationships with one another. He was persuaded that alternatives were available so long as human beings might have recourse to a science of association in the conceptualization and design of human institutions.[27]

To sum up, Vincent Ostrom noted, along with Tocqueville, that a certain "conceptual computational logic," that of citizenship, leads to a certain form of social order or governance. The emergence of that logic on a larger scale, and its related impact, is something relatively novel in history. With it, an alternative to other modes of governance is increasingly becoming possible, and a new reality of the noosphere may be created. The future of human civilization, Ostrom wrote, "will not just happen."[28] Citizenship implies an entirely new world of possibilities growing out of the specific "computational" and "combinatorial" logics specific to it.

Thus, on closer examination, the Ostroms' perspective on the problem of citizenship, civic capabilities, and civic studies is far from a mere corollary or footnote to their system. It is, in fact, part and parcel of their basic vision, a well-rounded perspective that encompasses an epistemological position, a political and institutional theory, a normative political economy, and even an ontology. That being said, it would be a mistake to claim that their system could or should be read only in this key, or that it could be reduced to an approach that pivots exclusively around it. However, to neglect the important positions citizenship, "civics," and their associated themes have in the Ostromian system would be an equally erroneous approach. As this chapter has tried to show, the theme of citizenship and civics is an important underlying theme of their work, and focusing on it opens interesting, novel, and potentially productive avenues.

NOTES

1. Vincent Ostrom, *The Meaning of Democracy and the Vulnerability of Democracies: A Response to Tocqueville's Challenge* (Ann Arbor, MI: University of Michigan Press, 1997), 271.
2. Elinor Ostrom, "Postscript: Challenging Institutional Analysis and Development," in *Challenging Institutional Analysis and Development: The Bloomington School,* ed. Paul D. Aligica and Peter J. Boettke (New York: Routledge, 2009), 159.
3. Ibid.
4. Vincent Ostrom, *The Meaning of Democracy,* 3.
5. Ibid., 271.
6. Ibid., 3.
7. Ibid.
8. Ibid., 271; see also Vincent Ostrom, "A Conceptual-Computational Logic for Federal Systems of Governance," in *Constitutional Design and Power-Sharing in the Post-Modern Epoch,* ed. D. J. Daniel (Lanham, MD: University Press of America, 1979), 19–20.
9. Vincent Ostrom, *The Meaning of Democracy,* 271.
10. Ibid., 294.
11. Ibid.
12. Ibid., 294–5; Vincent Ostrom, "Conceptual-Computational Logic," 14–15.
13. Ibid., 294.
14. Vincent Ostrom, "Conceptual-Computational Logic," 11.
15. Ibid., 20.
16. Ibid., 15.

17. Ibid.
18. Elinor Ostrom, "Beyond Positivism," in *Strategies of Political Inquiry*, ed. Elinor Ostrom (Beverly Hills, CA: Sage Publications, 1982), 16–17.
19. Vincent Ostrom, "Conceptual-Computational Logic," 18–19.
20. Ibid., 19.
21. Vincent Ostrom, *The Meaning of Democracy*, 294–5.
22. Ibid., 295.
23. Vincent Ostrom, "Conceptual-Computational Logic," 19.
24. Ibid.
25. Ibid.
26. Vincent Ostrom, *The Meaning of Democracy*, 291.
27. Vincent Ostrom, "Conceptual-Computational Logic," 20.
28. Vincent Ostrom, *The Meaning of Democracy*, 271.

PART 3 | Deliberative
Participation

5

Deliberative Civic Engagement: Connecting Public Voices to Public Governance

Tina Nabatchi and Greg Munno

DELIBERATIVE CIVIC ENGAGEMENT is an umbrella term for a wide variety of processes through which members of the public, often in concert with policy makers and stakeholders, devise solutions to public problems through democratic discussion. Although the idea of deliberation has deep historical roots, interest in deliberative ideals has waxed and waned over time. The last two decades have seen a deliberative revival, a resurgence of interest among scholars, practitioners, politicians, civic reformers, and others. Today, we find expressions of deliberative civic engagement in new constitutions, reform programs, and the resolutions of transnational movements and organizations; in the work of dozens of organizations committed to understanding, employing, and institutionalizing deliberation processes and programs; in research institutions at numerous colleges and universities; and in thousands of publications in a wide variety of academic disciplines.

This chapter explores deliberative civic engagement through a series of questions: What is deliberative civic engagement? Why does deliberative civic engagement matter? What does deliberative civic engagement look like in practice? Who is doing deliberative civic engagement, and why? What are the impacts and outcomes of deliberative civic engagement? And, what is the future of deliberative civic engagement? The goal in answering these questions is not to give exhaustive details, but rather to provide the broad brushstrokes needed to understand this rapidly developing area of civic studies.

WHAT IS DELIBERATIVE CIVIC ENGAGEMENT?

To understand deliberative civic engagement, it is useful to break the term into its two components. First, *deliberative* refers to a process characterized by deliberation, or the thoughtful and reasoned discussion of a problem based on facts, data, values, emotions, experiences, and ideas. Individuals often "deliberate" internally about issues of personal concern, but within the context of civic engagement, deliberation refers to a particular type of communication among a group of people who "carefully examine a problem and arrive at a well-reasoned solution after a period of inclusive, respectful consideration of diverse points of view."[1]

Second, *civic engagement* means working individually and collectively to develop the knowledge, skills, values, and motivations needed to identify and address issues of public concern. Civic engagement can happen in many places and can take different forms, from voluntarism to voting and from identifying community problems to taking collective action. At its heart lies the belief that individuals should be morally and socially responsible for promoting the quality of life in a community through both political and nonpolitical processes.

When these terms are joined, *deliberative civic engagement* denotes processes that enable citizens, civic leaders, and government officials to come together in public spaces where they can engage in constructive, informed, and decisive dialogue about important public issues. Put simply, deliberative civic engagement refers to inclusive and dynamic processes focused on public discovery, learning, and, ultimately, co-creation of solutions to common concerns.

WHY DOES DELIBERATIVE CIVIC ENGAGEMENT MATTER?

Advocates believe deliberative civic engagement is a potential remedy for what they see as the philosophical and practical shortcomings of current governmental practices. First, some are concerned about the inadequacies of representative democracy. They assert that while representative democracy is necessary and good, it is inadequate for democratic self-governance because, under the representative model, citizenship starts—and largely stops—at the voting booth. Moreover, voting occurs too infrequently, and there are few opportunities for meaningful public input on policy decisions between elections. This is problematic because consequential public policy decisions are not made based on citizen ideas and preferences, but rather on competitive pluralism wherein well-resourced and comparatively powerful factions or interest groups exert influence.

> *Deliberative civic engagement denotes processes that enable citizens, civic leaders, and government officials to come together in public spaces where they can engage in constructive, informed, and decisive dialogue about important public issues*

Second, other advocates are concerned that the ties among citizens and between citizens and government are deteriorating. They point to growing citizenship and democratic deficits to buttress their claim. The term *citizenship deficit* broadly refers to an erosion of civil society and civic engagement, and more specifically to an erosion of civic skills and dispositions among the general public. Evidence of a citizenship deficit is found in the falling levels of voter participation, voluntarism, trust in government, trust in media, and political efficacy, among other indicators. The term *democratic deficit* refers to the failure of government institutions to uphold and fulfill democratic principles. Evidence of a democratic deficit is found in the growing disconnect between citizens and policy makers, the gaps between citizen opinions and policy outcomes, and the frequent breakdown of government institutions.

Finally, some advocates point to more practical concerns about the apparent inability of government to address systemic policy problems, such as the impoverishment of educational attainment; disparities in access to and the quality of health care; the crumbling of transportation, utility, and other infrastructure systems; reductions in the supply of and access to energy; the mortgage crisis and the concomitant disintegration of housing markets; and the collapse of financial markets and the attendant problems of industry and business failure, unemployment, and the rise in the need for welfare and social services. As Mansuri and Rao note in chapter 6, the failed centralized development strategies of the 1970s and 1980s proved the folly of top-down approaches to these wicked problems. No wonder citizens are cynical: just as the true complexity of political, economic, social, and other problems are coming into focus, the attitudes and mechanisms of collective action needed to address those problems are disintegrating.

Because deliberative civic engagement embraces the premise that engaged citizenship is essential to the proper functioning of democratic government, it is argued to be a remedy for these and other problems. Advocates assert that deliberative civic engagement should be used as a supplement to (not a replacement for) representative democracy because it extends civic duties beyond the voting booth. Moreover, deliberative civic engagement moves away from competitive pluralism and encourages the deeper involvement of those who are (or will be) affected by a particular policy issue. It cultivates a broader conception of citizenship and a more active, inclusive, and vibrant public sphere where deliberation is the norm. In doing so, deliberative civic engagement also becomes a salve for citizenship and democratic deficits—it connects people to each other and to policy and decision makers; promotes the articulation, explanation, and justification of policy problems, options, and ultimate choices in terms of public values and the public good; and seeks to translate discussions into better public decisions and actions. In turn, the creation of lively public spaces where people can collectively and meaningfully discuss and make sense of shared problems and concerns fosters innovative thinking and develops public buy-in and action for the most pressing problems of our day. In short, advocates assert that deliberative civic engagement is a sensible and practical remedy for our current governance problems because it seeks to harness the power of citizens and policy makers to create—together—a deeper and more sophisticated understanding of public problems and potential responses. Whether deliberative civic engagement succeeds in living up to this potential is a complex and contested question, one that we explore later and one that Mansuri and Rao tackle in their chapter.

WHAT DOES DELIBERATIVE CIVIC ENGAGEMENT LOOK LIKE IN PRACTICE? Deliberative civic engagement is not a monolith. Rather, it is an umbrella term for a wide variety of approaches to public discussion. It includes dozens of "named," and sometimes even trademarked, processes (e.g., 21st Century Town Meetings, Citizens' Juries, Deliberative Polling, Study Circles, and National Issues Forums), as well as innumerable "unnamed" variations. These and other deliberative processes vary across many salient dimensions, including the following:[2]

- Sponsors and conveners. Processes can have a variety of sponsors (i.e., those who fund all or part of a direct engagement process) and conveners (i.e., those who plan and lead a direct engagement process), including an individual group or organization, a consortium of interested groups and organizations, one or more administrative officials representing one or more government agencies, or one or more elected officials.

- Purpose. Processes are used for many general reasons—to explore an issue and generate understanding, to resolve disagreements, to foster collaborative action, and to help make decisions, among others.
- Goals. Specific objectives can include informing participants, generating ideas, collecting data, gathering feedback, identifying problems, and making decisions.
- Size. The number of participants involved in a process can range from a few to hundreds or thousands; online processes could potentially involve millions.
- Participants. Some processes involve only expert administrators or professional or lay stakeholders, while others involve selected or diffuse members of the public.
- Participant recruitment. Processes may use self-selection, random selection, targeted recruitment, and/or incentives to bring people to the table.
- Participant preparation. Processes may or may not provide informational materials to better prepare participants for discussions.
- Locus of action. Some processes have intended actions or outcomes at the organizational or network level, whereas others seek actions and outcomes at the neighborhood, community, municipal, state, national, or even international level.
- Connection to policy process. Some processes are designed with explicit connections to policy and decision makers (at any of the loci listed above), while others have little or no connection to policy and decision makers, instead seeking to invoke individual or group action or change.
- Specificity of recommendations. Processes may produce a variety of outcomes, ranging from fairly generic to highly specific proposals or judgments.

Despite these differences, most deliberative civic engagement processes share some key features. First, they typically recruit a diverse body of participants who are or will be affected by a given issue. Second, they put participants in small groups (e.g., eight to ten people seated around a table), although the overall engagement is not necessarily limited in size. Finally, they engage participants in the process of deliberation, which provides everyone an adequate opportunity to speak, requires participants to listen respectfully to and consider the contributions of others, and generally proceeds through the following (often iterative) steps:

1. The creation of a solid information base about the nature of the problem at hand, often beginning with storytelling and the sharing of personal experiences
2. The identification, weighing, and prioritization of the values relevant to a given issue
3. The identification of a broad range of potential solutions to the problem
4. The weighing of the pros, cons, and trade-offs of the solutions through the systematic application of relevant knowledge and values to each alternative
5. The arrival at the best decision(s) or judgment(s) possible in light of what was learned through deliberation, which is sometimes followed by a planning process for action, implementation, and evaluation[3]

WHO IS DOING DELIBERATIVE CIVIC ENGAGEMENT, AND WHY?
Thousands of deliberative civic engagement processes are initiated across the United States and around the world each year.[4] The majority are convened at

the local level by elected officials, agency officials, individual groups or organizations, and consortiums of interested groups and organizations. As Mansuri and Rao explain in chapter 6, it is helpful to distinguish between "induced" and "organic" participatory processes. Participation is induced when processes are sponsored and convened by government, funders, and other official decision makers. Participation is "organic" when processes are sponsored and convened by civic groups acting independently of government. This distinction is very important, as there are often critical differences in the processes and outcomes of induced and organic processes.

Conveners use deliberative civic engagement for many reasons. Some espouse laudatory goals—for example, to promote the transparency, legitimacy, and fairness of policy-making processes and public decisions. This is particularly true of participation in the developing world, where in addition to providing political coverage and addressing the other concerns of conveners, sponsors such as the World Bank hope that deliberation can yield better outcomes, particularly for the least well off. As Mansuri and Rao write, "Underlying this shift [toward greater participation] was the belief that giving the poor a greater say in decisions that affected their lives, by involving them in at least some aspects of project design and implementation, would result in a closer connection between development aid and its intended beneficiaries." Despite these admirable aims, more often than not, conveners use deliberative civic engagement to achieve more concrete goals—for example, to generate support on a challenging issue, make decisions, get work done, and get closure.

For public officials, deliberative civic engagement is often used in reaction to frustrations with the policy-making process and to address difficult issues like school redistricting and closings, land use, the construction of highways or shopping malls, and other projects that lack political (and public) support or that bring decision-making bodies to an impasse. For example, decisions about city budgets, including raising revenues and cutting services, have prompted some local governments to use participatory budgeting, and concerns about the challenges of economic and sustainable development have led others to use deliberation for planning purposes. Sometimes, deliberative civic engagement is used in tough policy-making situations that require individual actions, behavioral changes, or small-group efforts on a large scale, as is found, for example, in race and diversity issues, crime and policing issues, and the involvement of parents in their children's education. Finally, deliberative civic engagement is sometimes used to quell voter backlash, as was done in Los Angeles, California, through the creation of a system of neighborhood councils and the Department of Neighborhood Empowerment.

Other times, deliberative civic engagement is used by civic leaders and civil society organizations (e.g., nonprofit, advocacy, or nongovernmental organizations) to help them pursue policy and structural changes, and to influence and transform the larger political process. As Matt Leighninger has observed, "Instead of continuing to push their agenda through lobbying, the media, or other established avenues within the political arena, these advocates are essentially trying to change the arena by bringing a larger number and wider array of people into the debate, and thus creating a deliberative environment where people can decide for themselves what they think should be done."[5] Projects that are initiated outside of government can be successful, particularly when they are able to activate a critical mass of voters.

Despite the broad use of deliberative civic engagement, processes are typically one-off experiments and "realized mainly as a temporary practice, a phenomenon experienced by citizens, public officials, and other leaders within the confines of a single issue over a short period of time."[6] Several factors contribute to the episodic use of deliberative civic engagement, including weak or inadequate legal infrastructures that prompt government officials to seek compliance with the explicit minimal standards for participation; the challenges of reaching scale and creating processes appropriate to the size of the political body; the need to overcome elements of the political system and political culture that are resistant to public engagement; and the lack of "civic assets" that connect citizens to one another and to their public institutions.

WHAT ARE THE IMPACTS AND OUTCOMES OF DELIBERATIVE CIVIC ENGAGEMENT?
Despite growing interest in deliberative civic engagement, serious debate continues about its benefits and limitations, particularly in terms of impacts and outcomes. Disagreement occurs not only between advocates and critics, but also between and among scholars and practitioners who support such work. Part of this disagreement stems from the fact that there are few comprehensive assessments of these practices and their consequences, although that is starting to change. One recent book, *Democracy in Motion,* investigates and integrates the diverse literature in a series of chapters designed to address specific practices or impacts of deliberative civic engagement. For concision, the findings of relevant chapters are discussed briefly below:

- As with other forms of political participation, several factors influence an individual's propensity to participate in deliberative civic engagement, including socioeconomic status, education, ideological intensity, and membership in social networks. Although people of higher socioeconomic status tend to be overrepresented in deliberative civic engagement processes, it is possible to increase diversity and representativeness by using random sampling, targeted recruitment, and/or various incentives.[7]
- Well-structured deliberative events generally produce high-quality discussion, even among diverse participants. Such events distinguish themselves from more commonplace public meetings with their emphasis on deliberative norms, trained facilitators, and concern about facing tradeoffs and finding common ground for issues and problems.[8]
- Deliberative civic engagement can help alleviate social problems such as exclusion, marginalization, and inequality when proactive design strategies are used, such as requiring the mandatory inclusion of diverse groups, providing adequate information to participants, using impartial moderators, adhering to standards of reciprocity and respect, using alternative modes of communication, and providing opportunity for consensual and concurrent decision making.[9]

- Online deliberative civic engagement can be an effective complement to face-to-face deliberation. It is more convenient and effective for certain tasks, such as brainstorming, and can aid group decision making when participants can hear and see each other in real time. There are, however, trade-offs: text-based, asynchronous deliberation may be less effective for fostering mutual understanding or changes in opinion, although it seems to compel broader participation and a greater variety of viewpoints.[10]
- Deliberative civic engagement can have educative effects for individual participants, particularly in terms of changing opinions and making opinions more informed, consistent, and durable. Deliberation can also change voting intentions and behaviors, and it can improve participants' civic attitudes such as political efficacy, political interests, trust in government, empathy, tolerance, and public spiritedness.[11]
- Deliberative civic engagement can help build community capacity by enhancing the sense of and commitment to community, the ability to solve problems, and access to resources. These outcomes may be increased if the deliberative process addresses issues of leadership, organizational development, community organizing, and collaboration.[12]
- Deliberative civic engagement sometimes results in short-, medium-, and long-term policy impacts, although evidence suggests that the connection between deliberative civic engagement and the policy-making process remains informal and dependent on the disposition of public officials and politicians to hear (and act upon) the recommendations that emerge in such forums. Moreover, the connection to policy making depends on the empowerment, embeddedness, and legitimacy of deliberative civic engagement, as well as on how recommendations are synthesized, made accessible, and fed into policy processes.[13]

In sum, when taken as a whole, there is a significant volume of literature showing that deliberative civic engagement can have advantages over other systems of governance. Among other benefits, it promotes deeper involvement by citizens in governance; thoughtful, informed, and reasoned debate of issues; respect for diverse viewpoints; and stronger policy decisions that have greater democratic legitimacy and effectiveness. However, such benefits are not universal, and several preconditions—inclusive designs, transparency, real opportunity to change outcomes, and so forth—are necessary if a deliberative engagement project is to have a desired outcome. In chapter 6, Mansuri and Rao identify other important caveats and make clear that bold claims that deliberative civic engagement can, on its own, address structural inequities and reverse generational poverty are almost always overstated. This is one reason why, despite the clear promise of deliberative civic engagement, the future of the field is still in question.

WHAT IS THE FUTURE OF DELIBERATIVE CIVIC ENGAGEMENT?

As noted earlier, interest in the theory and practice of deliberative civic engagement has varied over time. To ensure that the idea does not once again recede into the background, it is important to understand our current "deliberative moment," to embrace a vision of democracy that centers on citizen discussions of public issues, and to take action to make that vision a reality. Specifically, we need to understand the push for deliberative civic engagement and effectively respond by changing our views of citizens and citizenship, by addressing the problems of rhetorical advocacy, by finding ways to scale processes to meet the needs of large polities, and by building the civic infrastructure needed for citizens to participate in governance at all levels.

Certainly, one important push for more deliberative civic engagement is, at least in part, a response to the breadth, depth, and complexity of our modern challenges. We live in an era rife with wicked problems, intractable conflicts, and systemic policy failures at all levels of governance. These problems are exacerbated by mounting complexity, increasing interconnectedness, greater uncertainty, and growing environmental degradation, and by the escalating pace of social, economic, and political globalization. There is widespread agreement that these issues cannot be addressed without meaningful, purposeful, and efficacious government responses coupled with public buy-in and public action. Yet, at the same time, nations are struggling with citizenship and democratic deficits, crises of comity, declines in public resources, broken labor markets and economic systems, and moribund political and public support for policies and programs.

In light of these and other ailments, many have looked to deliberative civic engagement as a remedy. Yet, keeping the deliberative moment alive and enabling deliberative civic engagement to respond effectively to these issues requires changing how government and the public think about citizens and citizenship. Government must stop equating citizens with "the mob"; begin to understand that citizens can—and want to—engage in public work; and take advantage of shifts in the expectations and capacities of ordinary people. In turn, members of the public must rethink what it means to be a citizen; change how they conceptualize their roles, responsibilities, and relationships to government; and become more active in shaping the political destinies of their communities and nations. After all, distrust and displeasure with government—however legitimate—does not mean that citizens can turn away from government or that government can turn away from citizens. Indeed, the complexity of our problems simply demands that citizens and government work in concert.

Moreover, an effective response requires addressing the rhetorical problems of deliberative advocacy. Champions of deliberation must be aware of, and in some cases alter, the language they use to advance their cause. The challenge here is at least two-fold. First, most people outside the field do not know what deliberative civic engagement is, and when the idea is explained, politicians, government officials, citizens, and even some scholars doubt its practicality and viability. Second, deliberation is stereotyped as a "liberal" project, despite the fact that some of the most important deliberative innovations, such as the British Columbia Citizens' Assembly, came from the imaginations of right-of-center public officials and despite the fact that evidence of deliberation's aggregate impact on opinion does *not* suggest a left-leaning bias. In part, this is because of the language used to advance deliberative civic engagement. Deliberation is commonly associated with "liberal" or "left-leaning" terms and goals such as equality (of voice and opportunity), concern for the disenfranchised, and appeals to consensus and community. However, deliberation can also be articulated in "conservative" or "right-leaning" terms and goals, such as nongovernmental action, local authority, and the power of citizens to control public decisions and spending. Thus, advocates may want to reframe deliberation by balancing appeals for equality with appeals for individualism, noting the special recognition afforded to professional expertise, and highlighting the requirement of creating *informed* public voices, not just the shouts from the mob.

Keeping the deliberative moment alive also means finding ways to take deliberative civic engagement to scale. Those interested in democracy have long acknowledged that the scale, or size, of the political body matters for participation. Advocates, conveners, academics, civic reformers, and others must work together to better address the challenge of size and the concomitant challenge of costs. While information, communication, and other technological advances are rapidly making large-scale deliberative civic engagement cheaper and more viable, the field must embrace and capitalize on emerging technologies to bring processes to scale.

Finally, we must build the civic infrastructure needed for citizens to participate effectively in governance at every level. Such an infrastructure must include the creation of viable public spaces where citizens can meaningfully discuss issues, the cultivation of civic assets, and the building of a national network of conveners, facilitators, and other experts who can organize and support ongoing dialogue. It must be designed to educate citizens about important issues; to connect citizens to civic leaders, government officials, and other decision makers; to address the full governance cycle, from policy making to implementation to evaluation; and to make room not just for deliberation and decision making, but also for consistent, expedient, and purposeful action.

If we are able to address these issues and keep the deliberative civic engagement moment alive, then the future of this area of civic studies looks bright. Such work is particularly important now because deliberative civic engagement processes, if properly understood and implemented, could help effectively address the most complex social, political, and economic challenges of our time.

NOTES

1. John Gastil, *Political Communication and Deliberation* (Thousand Oaks, CA: Sage, 2008), 8.
2. This list of variations is adapted from Tina Nabatchi, "An Introduction to Deliberative Civic Engagement," in *Democracy in Motion: Evaluating the Practice and Impact of Deliberative Civic Engagement*, ed. T. Nabatchi, J. Gastil, M. Weiksner, and M. Leighninger (New York: Oxford University Press, 2012), 3–4; Nabatchi, *A Manager's Guide to Evaluating Citizen Participation* (Washington, DC: IBM Center for the Business of Government, 2012), 7; and Nabatchi, "Putting the 'Public' Back in Public Values Research: Designing Public Participation to Identify and Respond to Public Values," *Public Administration Review* 72, no. 5 (2012): 701–705.
3. Tina Nabatchi, "An Introduction to Deliberative Civic Engagement," in Nabatchi et al., *Democracy in Motion*, 8–9.
4. For examples, see the case studies available online at www.participedia.net.
5. Leighninger, "Mapping Deliberative Civic Engagement: Pictures from a (R)evolution," in Nabatchi et al., *Democracy in Motion*, 26.
6. Ibid., 24.

7. David M. Ryfe and Brittany Stalsburg, "The Participation and Recruitment Challenge," in Nabatchi et al., *Democracy in Motion*, 43–58.

8. Laura W. Black, "How People Communicate During Deliberative Events," in Nabatchi et al., *Democracy in Motion*, 59–80.

9. Alice Siu and Dragan Stanisevski, "Deliberation in Multicultural Societies: Addressing Inequality, Exclusion, and Marginalization," in Nabatchi et al., *Democracy in Motion*, 83–102.

10. Todd Davies and Reid Chandler, "Online Deliberation Design: Choices, Criteria, and Evidence," in Nabatchi et al., *Democracy in Motion*, 103–31.

11. Heather Pincock, "Does Deliberation Make Better Citizens?," in Nabatchi et al., *Democracy in Motion*, 135–62.

12. Bo Kinney, "Deliberation's Contribution to Community Capacity Building," in Nabatchi et al., *Democracy in Motion*, 163–80.

13. Gregory Barrett, Miriam Wyman, and Vera Schattan P. Coelho, "Assessing the Policy Impacts of Deliberative Civic Engagement: Comparing Engagement in the Health Policy Processes of Brazil and Canada," in Nabatchi et al., *Democracy in Motion*, 181–203.

The Challenge of Promoting Civic Participation in Poor Countries

6

Ghazala Mansuri and Vijayendra Rao

ONE IMPORTANT WAY to do civic studies is to assess democratic innovations in order to contribute to their success while also developing insights useful for other forms of civic work. In that spirit, the previous chapter reviewed research on deliberative democracy, with an emphasis on the developed world. Meanwhile, new approaches are being developed to promote the participation and voice of poor people in the development of their own communities. One such approach attempts to make participation by the poor an integral component of programs supported by international aid and finance organizations working in developing countries. An evaluation of these innovations provides another lens for understanding the civic process and thus for advancing civic studies.[1]

Over the course of the last two decades, the World Bank and other agencies tasked with improving economic development and reducing poverty in poor countries have spent over a hundred billion dollars to promote civic participation at the local level.[2] This is not the first time that the development community and governments have embraced the idea of participation. It has waxed and waned before. The current wave of interest in civic participation began as a reaction to the highly centralized development strategies of the 1970s and 1980s, which created a widespread perception among activists and nongovernmental organizations (NGOs) that "top-down" development was deeply disconnected from the needs of the poor. Underlying this shift was the belief that giving the poor a greater say in decisions that affect their lives, by involving them in at least some aspects of project design and implementation, would result in a closer connection between development aid and its intended beneficiaries.

Over the past decade, local participation has acquired a life of its own and is now proposed as a means to achieve a variety of goals—better poverty targeting, improved public service delivery, better maintained infrastructure, greater voice and social cohesion, and a more accountable and responsive government.

Achieving participatory governance and building civic capacity have historically been organic rather than state-led processes. By "organic" we mean spurred by civic groups acting independently of government, and often in opposition to it. Organic participation is usually driven by social movements aimed at confronting and reforming the structure of power, both in the private sector and within government. Such processes are often effective because they arise endogenously within a country's trajectory of change, and are often directed by highly motivated, charismatic leaders who mobilize citizens to give voice to their interests—their grievances, their rights, and their concerns—and can create or exploit political opportunities to achieve their goals. Organic participation is, therefore, a broad term. At one level, it includes participation in social movements that fight for greater democratic expression—such as the American civil rights movement and the anti-Apartheid movements—or labor movements that aim to unionize workers. The goal of such movements is ultimately to influence or transform the larger political process. At another level, organic participation includes participation in civic watchdog groups and in trade associations formed to represent the interests of particular industries. It also includes participation in cooperatives, such as the Self-Employed Women's Association in India; membership-based organizations that aim to improve livelihoods and living standards, such as the Grameen Bank in Bangladesh; and NGOs that seek to build citizenship and develop local communities through self-help, such as the Orangi Pilot Project in Pakistan. Organic participation, by its nature, implies a process of creative destruction. One must first imagine a world in which social and political relationships are more equitably arranged, or at least restructured in a manner congruent with the interests of the movement. Then this vision must be articulated with the goal of expanding influence and mobilizing citizens willing to support the cause, often at considerable personal cost.

When governments or nongovernmental organizations promote participation through policy actions implemented on a large scale, we call that "induced participation"

However, when governments or nongovernmental organizations promote participation through policy actions implemented on a large scale, we call that "induced participation."[3] There is often some overlap between organic and induced participation. Governments may decentralize because of the efforts of social movements, and the designs of induced participatory programs are often built on organic models. A government may decide to scale up the efforts of small-scale organic initiatives and thus turn them into induced development interventions. One important question is whether efforts initiated by organic participation can be scaled up by policy interventions in the form of projects. Rather than wait for the slow process of the organic development of civic capacity, can policy interventions speed up the process by harnessing the capacity of citizens to act collectively to accelerate development, and to improve the quality of government as well as the functioning of markets?

There are two major modalities for inducing local participation: the promotion of community development and the decentralization of resources and authority from national to local governments:

Community development refers to efforts to bring villages, urban neighborhoods, or other household groupings into the process of managing development resources without relying on formally constituted local governments.

Community development projects—variously labeled community-driven development, community-based development, community livelihood projects, and social funds—include efforts to expand community engagement in service delivery. Designs for this type of aid can range from community-based targeting, in which only the selection of beneficiaries is done through community engagement, to those where communities are involved to varying degrees in project design and management as well as the management of resources.

Decentralization refers to efforts to strengthen village and municipal governments on both the demand and supply sides. On the demand side, decentralization strengthens citizens' participation in local government by, for example, instituting regular elections, improving access to information, and fostering mechanisms for deliberative decision making. On the supply side, it enhances the ability of local governments to provide services by increasing their financial resources, strengthening the capacity of local officials, and streamlining and rationalizing their administrative functions.

The organic development of civic capacity is a complex process—deeply imbedded in a country's history, its internal conflicts, its conception of nationalism, its levels of education and literacy, the distribution of education and wealth, the nature of the state, the nature of economic and political markets, and a variety of other conditions. Importantly, organic participation is driven by self-motivated leaders who work tirelessly, with little compensation, and often at high personal cost—constantly innovating, networking, and organizing to get the movement to succeed. When this complex process of organic change, driven by intrinsically motivated people, is turned into policy—into projects and interventions that induce participation—it has to be transformed into manageable, bureaucratically defined entities with budgets, targets, and extrinsically motivated, salaried staff as agents of change. This transformation is common to all large-scale, state-led policy initiatives and has been characterized by James C. Scott as "seeing like a state."[4]

But civic interventions are different from other types of policy interventions in an important sense: encouraging greater participation can be quite threatening for those who enjoy privilege and power—including political agents, civil bureaucrats, and NGOs at the local level. Moreover, by devolving power to the local level, higher levels of government are giving away power, authority, and finances to communities over which they may have little control. Yet, those who stand to lose from a shift in the distribution of power are typically also charged with the implementation of participatory development projects and the organization of consultative bodies, like participatory councils, at both the central and the local levels. This suggests that project implementers need to be prepared to act against what may well be their own self-interest in promoting institutions whose purpose it is to upset the prevailing equilibrium. This presents an interesting conundrum that does not face organic movements.

In order to induce participation more effectively, in our view, several things need to be done at the World Bank and other donor agencies. We begin by a brief review of the available evidence on the effectiveness of participatory interventions and then lay out the basic shifts in approach and implementation that we see as necessary for a more effective mobilization of citizens in the development process.

REVIEWING THE EVIDENCE

In a recently completed book, we synthesize the available evidence on the effectiveness of induced participatory projects.[5] In this section, we take up some of the more salient points in order to illustrate our main argument regarding the challenges of induced participation.

We begin with the questions that are at the heart of efforts to "go local": Do participatory programs enhance the involvement of the poor and the marginalized in community-level decision-making bodies, and does this increase "voice"? Do participatory programs result in budget allocations or spending decisions that are more closely aligned with the preferences of community members? Who speaks for a community, and who benefits from local resource allocation? In particular, does community engagement reduce the appropriation of program benefits by local elites, often called "elite capture," and does it ultimately create more resilient and inclusive local institutions?

On balance, we find that participants in civic activities are more likely to be male and tend be wealthier, more educated, of higher social status (by caste and ethnicity), and more politically connected than nonparticipants. This may reflect, to a degree, the higher opportunity cost of participation for the poor. There is some evidence that the poor spend both less time and less money—as one might expect—on collective activities. There is also some evidence that the poor attend community meetings in larger numbers when they stand to benefit directly by doing so—usually because beneficiaries for targeted programs are selected in such meetings.

However, it also appears that the poor, regardless of incentives to participate, tend to benefit less from participatory processes. For one thing, resource allocation decisions typically reflect the preferences of elite groups. Whether or not this distorts the pro-poor intent of programs, then, depends quite substantially on community characteristics. Studies from a variety of countries show that high-inequality communities do much worse, especially when there is a concentration of political, economic, and social power in the hands of a few. Capture also tends to be greater in communities that are remote from centers of power; have low levels of literacy; have high levels of poverty; or have significant caste, race or gender disparities. Policy design can have unintended consequences; there is some evidence that a large injection of resources can induce greater participation by the wealthy and increase exclusion.

In sum, in the absence of explicit and enforceable rules of affirmative inclusion, a few wealthy and often politically well-connected men—who are not necessarily more educated than other participants—tend to make decisions at community meetings. Some studies find, moreover, that civic organizations tend to self-sort into those led and attended by the wealthy and those attended by the poor. This may serve to create organizations of the poor that remain weak and vulnerable and, therefore, undermine the goal of social cohesion.

The potential for resource capture by political elites is often no less worrying than the privately motivated activities of traditional elites. There is plenty of evidence that local politicians use public budgets to reward political allies and loyal constituents, to improve their own future electoral outcomes, and to increase their private fortunes. The ultimate question of interest, though, is whether the overall scope for capture is dampened under democratic decentralization. The answer appears to be a cautiously optimistic one. Available studies suggest that, under democratic decentralization, spending decisions are better aligned with local needs. There is also a shift of resources in favor of the less advantaged. However, much depends on the nature of electoral incentives and the capacity of higher levels of government to provide oversight and to ensure downward accountability.

Ultimately, the impetus for most participatory projects, as well as for decentralization, is the hope that greater engagement by citizens will lead to a faster and more inclusive development process. We now assess the extent to which participation improves the targeting of antipoverty projects, enhances the delivery of public services, increases incomes, and leads to better management of natural resources and better maintenance of infrastructure. We also try to identify, as far as the literature permits, the channels through which community engagement improves outcomes and the factors that appear to limit its effectiveness.

Studies that have looked at the relative gain from decentralized targeting find that local agents are often able to target beneficiary households better than centrally driven schemes. However, it appears that the gains tend to be small. There is also considerable evidence that communities and individuals who get left out tend to be poorer and less well connected to relevant political networks. They also tend to be the least literate. Areas that are remote, poorly served by media, or disadvantaged in terms of infrastructure quality also tend to have worse targeting outcomes.

We turn next to the role of community participation in improving the delivery of public services like health and schooling. Efforts to engage communities in improving basic health services or primary schools are now pervasive, and the evidence for community engagement is also, on the whole, more heartening— though there are some caveats. First, efforts to engage communities in improving basic health services or primary schools are usually multifaceted interventions that also involve a substantial injection of funds. This makes it difficult to isolate the impact of community engagement, and most studies don't even try to do so. However, a handful of randomized evaluations of community-based health programs are an important exception. These evaluations find that while greater community engagement alone is not sufficient for improving any health outcome, community participation can be quite beneficial where projects also provide trained health personnel at the community level or make investments in upgrading health facilities. Projects achieve the greatest improvements under these conditions— delivering substantial reductions in maternal and infant mortality, greater use of health facilities, and significant modification of health behaviors. These results suggest that community participation may well account for at least some of the positive health effects observed in less well identified studies.

Community engagement in education has had similar impacts in some respects, though the evidence is more varied and the effects more muted. Overall, studies report an increase in school access and enrollment as well as improvements in retention rates, student attendance, and promotion to higher grades. However, the impact on student learning tends to be weak. This may be due, at least in part, to the relatively short evaluation periods of most studies. The typical time period associated with improvements in learning is approximately eight years, while the bulk of studies completed to date look at impacts within the first two to three years. Weak learning impacts may also be due to greater school access and the consequent entry of children from underprivileged backgrounds who tend to be less prepared for school. In fact, some studies do show a worsening in average learning outcomes, which tend to disappear or diminish considerably when new enrollment is accounted for.

As with other interventions, though, poorer and more remote areas are less able to realize gains from decentralized service delivery. Localities also do worse when they are less well administered and more embedded within a nexus of corruption, with poor democratic practices and a politicized administration. Low literacy levels impose a further constraint. Several studies find that low literacy levels make it harder for communities to participate in decentralized programs and to make informed decisions when they do.

Community-based development projects are often promoted as a tool to eradicate poverty. This is an area where the evidence is most mixed and is largely negative—though the diversity of interventions and the lack of rigorous studies make it difficult to draw clear conclusions. That said, most carefully done studies find that participatory antipoverty projects have had little impact on income poverty. The studies that find some positive impact on income, savings, or assets also tend to find that gains are observed only for the wealthy or only during the lifecycle of the project. When sustainable gains are realized, they are confined to specific sub-groups—such as the more educated among the poor—who are not the largest beneficiaries of the program being evaluated.

Next, we turn to the question that is at the core of the participatory approach to development: in what ways do participatory efforts seek to confront and repair civic failures, and how successful have these efforts been? We look at efforts to build social cohesion, in conditions of peace as well as in the aftermath of conflict; efforts to redress entrenched social inequalities of caste, ethnicity, and gender through explicit inclusion mandates; and the creation of participatory forums where collective decisions can be made in a deliberative manner or where, at the very least, the exercise of "voice" can be practiced and refined.

There is little evidence that induced participation builds long-lasting cohesion, even at the community level. Group formation tends to be both parochial and unequal. What seems to happen instead is that during the course of a project, people are induced to participate and build networks. But they do so in order to benefit from the cash and other material payoffs provided by the project, an effect that tends to melt away when the incentives are withdrawn. One indication of this is that the observed impacts of participation tend to be in response to attitudinal questions about the "role of the community in development" or whether "the community can achieve things on its own." Impacts are not, however, seen in broader attitudes toward democracy or in objective measures of collective action. Only when projects explicitly link community-based organizations with markets or provide skills training do they tend to improve group cohesiveness and collective action beyond the life of the project.

With these caveats in mind, there is some heartening evidence that participation has intrinsic value. Communities tend to express greater satisfaction with decisions they help make even when participation in the decision-making process does not change the outcome or where outcomes are not consistent with their expressed preferences.

On the whole, however, the ballot box, though far from perfect, provides a clearer mechanism for sanctioning unpopular policy choices by traditional or political elites, as compared to more informal forums for deliberation. In decentralized settings, electoral incentives—credible and open elections—tend to help by aligning the decisions of politicians with the demands of their constituencies. Moreover, in such settings, we find that participatory and deliberative councils, when they exist, can foster a significant degree of civic engagement. It is less clear how citizens can collectively sanction negligent or corrupt officials or local leaders where such venues for the exercise of voice are not available.

Repairing civic failures also requires that social inequalities be addressed. One way of trying to do so is to mandate the inclusion of disadvantaged groups in the participatory process. Evaluations of community-driven development projects provide virtually no evidence about whether this works. However, a growing body of evidence from village democracies in India indicates broadly positive impacts. Quotas in village councils and presidencies for disadvantaged groups and women tend to change political incentives in favor of the group that is privileged by the quota.

Mandated inclusion also appears to provide an incubator for new political leadership. Evidence indicates that women and other excluded groups are more likely to stand for office for non-mandated seats once they have had some experience holding a mandated seat. Quotas can also weaken prevailing stereotypes that assign low ability and poor performance to traditionally excluded groups. However, lasting change requires that the inclusion mandates remain in place for long enough to change perceptions and social norms.

It is less clear that community-based projects, which are typically ad hoc and temporary, can induce similar shifts in attitudes, opportunities, and political dynamics. Decentralized programs usually have a constitutional mandate or other legal sanction from the center and are relatively permanent. They may thus be better able to affect change by shifting social and political dynamics over the long term. More evidence is needed on this important question.

To sum up, three lessons appear to be abundantly clear. First, context, both local and national, is extremely important. Outcomes from interventions are highly variable across communities. Inequality, history, geography, the nature of social interactions, networks, and political systems all have a strong influence. Thus, a successful project designed for one context may fail miserably in another. This suggests the need for strong in-built systems of learning and monitoring, great sensitivity to context, and a willingness and ability to adapt. As some of the evidence shows, carefully designed projects, whether they are implemented by governments or by donor-funded implementing agencies, are able to limit the negative impact of "bad" community characteristics, at least to a degree.

Second, the idea that all communities have a ready stock of "social capital" that can simply be harnessed is naïve in the extreme. Instead, all the evidence suggests that building citizenship, which includes engaging communities in monitoring service providers and governments and supporting community-based management of natural resources or infrastructure, requires a serious and sustained engagement in efforts to build local capacity.

Finally, third, induced participatory interventions work best when they are supported by a responsive state. While local actors may have an informational and locational advantage, they appear to use it to the benefit of the disadvantaged only where institutions and mechanisms to ensure local accountability are robust. In fact, local oversight is most effective when other, higher level institutions of accountability function well and when communities have the capacity to effectively monitor service providers and others in charge of public resources. This appears to increase, rather than diminish, the need for functional and strong institutions at the center.

Agencies that implement donor-funded projects need to have the capacity to exercise adequate oversight. However, there is little evidence that donors alone can substitute for a nonfunctional state as a higher-level accountability agent. When funds are parachuted down into communities without any monitoring by a supportive state, decision making is more susceptible to capture by elites who control the local cooperative infrastructure, which, in turn, leads to a high risk of corruption. Instead, reforms that enhance judicial oversight, allow for independent audit agencies, and protect and promote the right to information and a free media appear to be necessary for effective local participation.

In this, our findings are consistent with the large body of case-study evidence of what Jonathan Fox described, many years ago, as a "sandwich movement" of enlightened state action from above interacting with social mobilization from below.[6] The state does not necessarily have to be democratic—though that helps a great deal—but in the sphere where the intervention is being conducted, at the level of the community or the neighborhood, the state has to be responsive to community demands. For example, schools that involve parents in making decisions will be more responsive to the demands of those parents if the parents have a measure of control over school budgets. And village governments become more responsive to the needs of citizens when they function within an electoral democracy supplemented by deliberative interactions.

This is not to say that participatory engagement cannot make a difference in the absence of a supportive state under all circumstances. It can, but usually when that engagement is organic and thus outside of, and often in resistance to, the state.

DONORS, GOVERNMENTS, AND TRAJECTORIES OF CHANGE
A major problem with donor-induced participation is that it works within what might be described as an "infrastructure template." The institutional

structure and incentives of donor organizations are optimally suited to projects with short timelines, linear trajectories of change, and clear, unambiguous projected outcomes. When a bridge is built, the outcome is easily verified, the trajectory of change is predictable, and the impact is almost immediate. This is not the case with participatory interventions that engage in the much more complex task of shifting political and social equilibria which can have very different trajectories.

Unfortunately, however, most participatory projects that emerge from donor agencies are designed with the same assumed trajectory as infrastructure projects. They are also forced to work within three- or five-year cycles and are approved on the belief that, at the end of those cycles, various civic objectives will have been reached—such as higher levels of social cohesion, community empowerment, improved accountability, etc. Almost all community-driven projects go further in projecting gains in outcomes such as reduction of poverty, increases in school enrollments, improvements to sanitation and health, etc. The assumption is that, within the period of the project cycle, the intervention will activate civic capacity to the extent required to begin to repair political and market failures and have an observable impact on "hard" outcomes. Three beliefs underlie this assumption: The first is that civic engagement will be activated in the initial period of the project. The second is that civic capacity will be deepened enough to repair government and market failures. And the third is that any improvement in the quality of governments and markets will result in a measurable change in outcomes.

Figure 1 illustrates the problems with these beliefs. The dotted lines indicate an immediate and linear response of both civil society and governance outcomes and a congruent change in measurable economic development outcomes. The problem with this reasoning is that civic change is a highly unpredictable process. Consider the kinds of things that have to take place in order to achieve civic change. Individuals have to believe that collective mobilization is worth the effort and be willing to participate; civic groups have to solve the collective-action problem

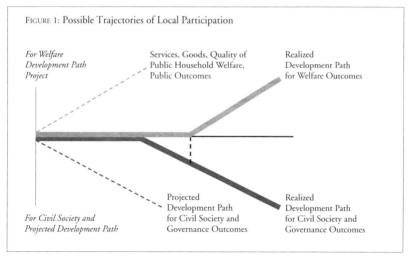

FIGURE 1: Possible Trajectories of Local Participation

For Welfare Development Path Project

Services, Goods, Quality of Public Household Welfare, Public Outcomes

Realized Development Path for Welfare Outcomes

Projected Development Path for Civil Society and Governance Outcomes

Realized Development Path for Civil Society and Governance Outcomes

For Civil Society and Projected Development Path

and exploit political opportunities to effect change; the nexus of accommodation in government has to be disrupted by the rising cost of ignoring citizens' interests, so that politicians and bureaucrats change their actions; and the new actions of politicians and bureaucrats have to result in changed outcomes. In other words, a change in outcomes has to be preceded by an improvement in civic capacity, and this improvement has then to unleash a series of further changes that will affect outcomes.[7] The reality is depicted in figure 1 by the solid lines.

Predicting when change will meaningfully occur in each of the nodes in figure 1 is extremely difficult, because a number of factors come into play: the degree of cooperative capacity; the history of civic engagement and politics; the level of development; the extent to which the state has committed to the process of change and is, therefore, effectively incentivizing, enforcing, and monitoring the actions of its agents; the level of literacy; information flows—in other words, everything that affects civic success. Social equilibrium is hard to change because it evolves over years of repeated interactions within a particular economic, political, and social environment.

Furthermore, until citizens are convinced that the high cost of engaging—of fighting for their interests and resisting elite domination—is worth the effort, change in the social equilibrium is unlikely to happen in an effective manner. Widespread participation occurs when a tipping point is reached—when enough people are convinced of the value of participation, when they sense a fundamental change in the nature of politics and power, and when enough people have convinced enough others, resulting in a participatory cascade. Thus, induced participation—particularly when it is packaged within a project—is almost set up for failure due to unrealistic predictions that emerge from bureaucratic imperatives. The challenge for those who design policy interventions is to figure out where each community is within this complex trajectory of change and to create an enabling environment for that change to occur in a manner that improves development objectives. For induced participatory projects to have a chance of meeting their objectives, the spirit of experimentation, learning, and persistent engagement that characterizes organic participatory change will need to be built into both their design and implementation. Unfortunately, donors are often bound by strict timelines, imperatives to disperse money both quickly and effectively, and internal incentives that make honest and effective monitoring and evaluation a low priority at the project level. In the following section, we look at incentives to evaluate and monitor in participatory projects funded by the World Bank, which has made important strides in improving project-based evaluations over the past decade or so.

MONITORING AND ATTENTION TO CONTEXT IN WORLD BANK PROJECTS
The variability of local context highlights the importance of developing effective monitoring systems in large participatory projects. Such projects require constant adjustment, learning in the field, and experimentation in order to be effective. A notable example of an effectively monitored, induced community development project is the $1.3 billion Kecamatan Development Program (KDP)

in Indonesia, which was active for ten years between 1998 and 2008. KDP provided block grants directly to rural community-based organizations to fund development plans prepared through a participatory process. In this it was very similar to a large number of other community-based projects. Where KDP differed was in the extent to which it relied on context-specific design and attention to monitoring systems.[8]

KDP's design was based on two key elements: (1) a careful analysis of existing state and community capacity drawn from a set of studies of local institutions; and (2) a deep understanding of the history of community development in Indonesia. Implementation involved creating a tiered network of motivated and trained facilitators who created a feedback loop to facilitate learning and worked with engineers to supervise the quality of construction of village infrastructure financed through a block grant. Villagers took control of expenditures and procured goods and services on a competitive basis. They also formed monitoring teams that checked the delivery of material and the quality of construction and reported their findings to the village forum. In addition to participatory monitoring, audits were conducted at the sub-district (Kecamatan) level by project implementers. Moreover, independent NGOs and journalists were contracted to monitor and report on the quality of the project on a random basis. These innovations in monitoring were supplemented with more conventional quantitative tools, such as a carefully designed management information system, several qualitative and quantitative evaluations, and case studies.[9] Most importantly, the project emphasized an honest system of communication, which allowed observations—both critical and complementary—to constantly inform innovations in design and implementation.

Unfortunately, KDP is among a very small group of World Bank–funded participatory projects that have made an effort to build effective monitoring systems. We reviewed the monitoring and evaluation systems in place in participatory projects funded by the World Bank between 1999 and 2007.[10] In our review, we examined a range of project documents, including the Project Appraisal Document (PAD), which is among the main documents assessed by the World Bank's executive board before approving a loan. The PAD lays out project design, relevance, expected outcomes and implementation and rollout plans. It should also include a detailed account of the plans for monitoring and evaluating the project. We also looked at implementation status reports and implementation completion reports (ICRs) for a random sample of 20 percent of these projects in order to assess the effectiveness of proposed monitoring and evaluation systems in the PAD. An ICR is typically prepared by the project manager after every supervision mission. Implementation status reports, prepared by project teams, are screened by the Independent Evaluation Group at the World Bank. Finally, we assessed information from project supervision documents that synthesize the results of regular project visits by Bank operational task teams. Our analysis also encompassed a survey of project managers ("task team leaders," in World Bank parlance), to gather information that was not available in project documents.

The PADs were striking in their similarity. Often, their language was cut-and-pasted from one project to the next, suggesting a singular lack of attention to context. The documents and the survey also revealed pervasive inattention to monitoring systems. Only 40 percent of PADs included a monitoring system as an essential part of the project design, and a third contained no mention of basic monitoring requirements, such as a management information system. When monitoring was mentioned, it usually involved collecting extremely imprecise indicators, and even this was done irregularly. The most important reasons given for the paucity of effective monitoring were poor human and technical capacity and a lack of sufficient funding. On the crucial question of whether monitoring and evaluation data are a guide to "learning by doing," only 14 percent of the project documents explicitly outlined procedures that would be implemented if the monitoring and evaluation data indicated that a project had gone off track.

The majority of project managers participating in our survey stated that the Bank's operational policies do not provide any incentives for effective monitoring and evaluation. While most believe that monitoring and evaluation are stated priorities for the Bank's senior management, they also believe that, in practice, this is not the case. Project managers highlighted several major constraints, from an institutional perspective, that limit investments in effective monitoring and evaluation systems. The majority (75 percent) believe that the Bank's operational policies do not provide the right incentives to engage in systematic monitoring and evaluation. Further, a majority (66 percent) of project managers believe that Bank monitoring and evaluation requirements and Bank supervision budgets are not tailored to project size, project complexity, or country context. Finally, only a third believe that the standard timeframe for projects (an average of 5.5 years) is sufficient for realizing participatory objectives.

An open and effective monitoring and evaluation system requires a tolerance for risk, flexible project design, and adequate resources. These conditions seem to be absent for the most part. A major problem, highlighted by the survey respondents, along with lack of management support, was the lack of an adequate project supervision budget. Most task managers also believe that governments see monitoring systems as a box to be checked in order to qualify for a loan, rather than as an instrument to improve the effectiveness of projects. Given the belief that country counterparts have little incentive to implement good monitoring and evaluation systems, explicit support from the Bank may be all the more critical.

CONCLUSION

We do not believe that the vision articulated by Amartya Sen and others of a more inclusive, deliberative and participatory form of development is an idealistic dream.[11] We are hopeful that, with significant changes in structures and incentives within development agencies, induced participatory development can be made much more effective. There is some evidence that things can change.

However, local participation does not work when it is merely the ad hoc, myopically directed creation of a project. It works when it has teeth, when it builds on organic movements, when it is facilitated by a responsive center, when it is adequately and sustainably funded, and when interventions are conditioned by a culture of learning by doing. This requires a flexible, long-term approach informed by careful political, social and economic analysis, and the willingness to adapt both project design and expected outcomes if required.

Monitoring systems also need to be taken far more seriously. For one thing, projects need clear systems of facilitator feedback and effective participatory monitoring and redress systems. The use of new and more cost-effective tools, such as reporting by text messaging, could assist greatly in this effort. The effort to evaluate projects carefully also needs to be scaled up considerably with far more attention to unpacking the mechanisms or channels through which change is expected to occur. Most importantly, there needs to be a tolerance for honest feedback to facilitate learning, instead of a tendency to rush to judgment coupled with a pervasive fear of failure. The complexity of participatory development requires, if anything, a higher tolerance for failure. This, in turn, requires a change in the mindset of management and clear incentives that encourage project leaders to investigate what does and does not work in their projects and to report on it.

Instead of focusing entirely on inducing participation, policy makers would also be well served by thinking through effective ways to ride waves of organic participation. This can be done by inviting civic activists to help design and monitor participatory projects, by creating an enabling environment for civic activists to be agents of change, by creating spaces for public deliberation in local governments, and by working with governments to create incentives for agents of government to be responsive to the needs of citizens.

In 2004, in a review of the literature on participatory development, we found a singular lack of attention to both monitoring and evaluation.[12] Eight years later, we find that the gap in evaluations has been addressed to some extent, but that the lack of attention to monitoring, unfortunately, persists. This is coupled with inflexible institutional rules that do not internalize the complexity inherent in engaging with civic-led development. The ignorance of context in design is another major problem. If this situation is addressed, we believe that participatory development projects could become much more effective.

NOTES

1. A detailed theoretical exposition of these ideas and a comprehensive review of the evidence can be found in Ghazala Mansuri and Vijayendra Rao, *Localizing Development: Does Participation Work?* (Washington, DC: World Bank, 2013); Mansuri and Rao, "Can Participation be Induced? Evidence from Developing Countries," *Critical Review of International Social and Political Philosophy* 16, no. 2 (2013): 284–304.

2. $85 billion from the World Bank (Mansuri and Rao 2012), with far more coming in from other donors such as US Agency for International Development, the UK's Department for International Development, etc. For information about the core mission of the World Bank, see http://www.worldbank.org/about. Information about the World Bank's approach to participation is available at: http://www.worldbank.org/en/topic/socialdevelopment.

3. (See Mansuri and Rao, 2012 for a discussion of the concept of "induced participation.)

4. Scott, J. 1999. *Seeing Like a State: How Certain Schemes to Improve the Human Condition Have Failed.* New Haven, CT: Yale University Press.

5. Ghazala Mansuri and Vijayendra Rao, *Localizing Development: Does Participation Work?* (Washington, DC: World Bank, 2012). In this World Bank policy research report, we review

over five hundred studies, focusing at greater length on large-scale participatory projects that have been evaluated using representative samples of target populations with good counterfactuals. While much of the literature on participation tends to use a case-study approach, which is undoubtedly quite invaluable for understanding the process of change, only representative sample studies of large-scale projects with good counterfactuals can generate enough data to make statistically valid judgments on large-scale policy interventions. In other words, we focus on studies that have a valid control group for the communities that have been targeted (or "treated") by the intervention. Without an adequate counterfactual, there is no effective way of attributing the observed changes to the intervention rather than to changes that might have occurred outside the intervention. Generally speaking, this means that our findings derive from econometric analysis. However, we do draw on several case studies to develop ideas and to illustrate our conceptual framework. Ideally, this econometric work should be complemented by good qualitative work, which would help illuminate the processes that resulted in the observed impact. There is an unfortunate dearth of such work. We refer the reader to the book for a detailed synthesis of the evidence and the bibliography.

6. Jonathan Fox, *The Politics of Food in Mexico: State Power and Social Mobilization* (Ithaca, NY: Cornell University Press, 1993).
7. Michael Woolcock, "Toward a Plurality of Methods in Project Evaluation: A Contextualized Approach to Understanding Impact Trajectories and Efficacy," *Journal of Development Effectiveness* 1 (2009), 1–14.
8. Scott Guggenheim, "The Kecamatan Development Project, Indonesia," in *The Search for Empowerment: Social Capital as Idea and Practice at the World Bank*, ed. A. Bebbington, S. Guggenheim, E. Olson, and M. Woolcock (Hartford, CT: Kumarian Press, 2006).
9. Susan Wong, "Indonesia Kecamatan Development Program: Building a Monitoring and Evaluation System for a Large-scale Community-Driven Development Program," Discussion Paper, World Bank, Washington, DC, 2003.
10. Mansuri and Rao, *Localizing Development*, Chapter 7.
11. See Amartya Sen, *Development as Freedom* (New York: Knopf, 1999).
12. Ghazala Mansuri and Vijayendra Rao, "Community-Based and -Driven Development: A Critical Review," *World Bank Research Observer* 19, no.1 (2004): 1–39.

PART 4 | Public Work

7

Transforming Higher Education in a Larger Context: The Civic Politics of Public Work

Harry C. Boyte and Blase Scarnati

THE FRAMING STATEMENT for civic studies, entitled "The New Civic Politics," emphasizes two fundamental themes: *agency* and *co-creation*.[1] Agency can be understood as a form of empowerment that has conscious political dimensions, or as effective and intentional action that is conducted in diverse and open settings in order to shape the world around us. Co-creation refers to "public work," a framework of theory and practice that informed the statement. In what follows, we argue that the new civic politics of public work differs from the moralizing and polarizing approaches to "politics" commonly found in and beyond the academy today. The politics of public work opens possibilities for building broad alliances across partisan and other divides. Practicing such politics will enable us to become agents and architects, not objects, of change.

The need for agency and co-creation is pervasive at the beginning of the twenty-first century. American colleges and universities offer just one example. David Scobey sees an academy "in the throes of change, even revolution.... [T]he question is not *whether* the academy will be changed, but *how*." Scobey predicts that "the knowledge, skills, and values in which students should be educated; the intellectual landscape of disciplines and degrees; the ways in which educational institutions are organized; the funding of teaching, learning, and research" will all "be profoundly different in twenty years." He also observes that the forces of change result from "our own inertia," as well as "broad political, market, and technological developments not of our making."[2]

Inertia grows from a pervasive sense of powerlessness in the face of dramatic transformation. Many in higher education have a critical understanding of the forces and trends that are rapidly changing our institutions. They are aware that legislatures are cutting state funding for public institutions; for-profit colleges are growing; publics are skeptical about institutional missions; and many administrators are deemphasizing liberal education in an effort to be more directly relevant to workforce needs—with little attention to the radically changing nature of work and workplaces, or to the leadership roles that higher education needs to play in addressing such change.

Yet, critique does not often lead to productive action. We propose that the new civic politics, a politics of public work, can both generate hope and build our capacity for *making* change in higher education and beyond.

PUBLIC WORK

Today, it is common for public and civic institutions—whether governments, schools, colleges, or nonprofits—to conceive of citizens as customers pursuing their own narrow interests. Those who promote deliberative democracy expand this narrow view, seeing citizens as talkers and judges about the common good. But both perspectives assume that the basic structure of society is a given. In contrast to both, the concept of public work highlights what can be called "world building," to borrow a term coined by the late political theorist Hannah Arendt. We take world building to refer to the role of citizens as *co-creators,* rather than simply *participants,* of the world we share in common.[3]

Public work can be defined as self-organized efforts by a mix of people who create goods, material or symbolic, whose civic value is determined through an ongoing process of deliberation. It has roots in communal labor practices around the world that create and sustain "the commons"—shared resources of all kinds, from fisheries to wells and from schools to public arts. The hallmarks of public work include self-organizing, egalitarian, and cooperative efforts by people who would otherwise be divided; practical concern for creating shared collective resources; adaptability; and incentives based on appeals to immediate interests combined with cultivation of concern for long-term community well-being. As we will show later, the public work framework also draws from social movements like populism that combine efforts to promote large-scale democratization with efforts to build broad political alliances. The concept of public work highlights the public and civic dimensions of many kinds of *work* that often are not recognized by conventional approaches to civic engagement, and it also highlights the practices that flow from distinctly civic identities—e.g., citizen teachers, citizen businesspersons, citizen health professionals, citizen beauticians, and "civil servants" who see themselves as citizens working with other citizens.

> *Public work can be defined as self-organized efforts by a mix of people who create goods, material or symbolic, whose civic value is determined through an ongoing process of deliberation*

A RETURN TO POLITICS

Public work is political in the root sense of the word "politics," which is derived from the Greek word *polis,* meaning "city," and which, according to Aristotle, conveys plurality. In this sense of politics, people have diverse interests and perspectives and must express their contrary views, make decisions, allocate resources, select leaders, form alliances, and take various kinds of action.[4]

An obstacle to public work in our time is a narrow understanding of politics as a zero-sum competition among professional politicians—or as an equally zero-sum struggle between good and evil, the righteous in battle against evildoers. Because these forms of conflict are unattractive, many citizens have turned away from politics. Reform efforts often aim to institute markets, administrative systems, or scientific processes that will make such politics unnecessary. William Galston described "the decades-long reign of what some have called 'high liberalism'

[as] a desire to evade, displace, or escape from politics."[5] Bonnie Honig observed, and lamented, a similar pattern: "Those writing from diverse positions—republican, liberal, and communitarian—converge in their assumptions that . . . the task . . . is to resolve institutional questions, to get politics right, over and done with, to free modern subjects and their sets of arrangements [from] political conflict and instability."[6]

In contrast, public work insists on an understanding of politics as a practical approach to making change through negotiation, bargaining, and accommodation of diverse interests. As Stephen Elkin put it, "There is no substitute for politics . . . the various ways in which we arrive at collective, authoritative decisions in a world in which people legitimately hold different views. . . ."[7] Elkin founded *The Good Society*, a journal with a strong orientation to civic studies that embodies realist politics. Journal articles address such problems as disparities in economic and political power, environmental damage, welfare dependency, growing bureaucratization, and political alienation. And they explore workable models for social arrangements that embody such values as liberty, democracy, equality, and environmental sustainability. The journal is also highly skeptical of sweeping ideologies and utopian blueprints.

The challenge in adopting any of these ideas is that citizenship has shrunk like the Cheshire cat in *Alice in Wonderland*. With that shrinking, the power to make change has eroded. "Customers" have replaced civic producers.

Shrinking citizenship

While calls for the revitalization of civic education and civic learning have multiplied, civic learning remains on the margins. Today, as the following story illustrates, citizenship is understood as government-centered acts (like voting or contacting elected officials) plus off-hours voluntarism detached from work identities and work sites. A story illustrates.

When the Center for Democracy and Citizenship (CDC) at Augsburg College partnered with the City of Falcon Heights, Minnesota, to organize a moderated "citizen town hall" meeting that explored citizen-based approaches to gun violence, the audience of twenty-five or so included the mayor, the police chief, the city manager, teachers, a local principal, social agency workers, four students, business entrepreneurs, and two elderly residents. The residents expressed regret that "there are so few citizens" present. No one from any of the community work sites questioned this choice of words. However, by noting that all the participants actually *were* citizens, CDC staff prompted a lively conversation about what the community would look like if work sites were understood as citizenship sites, and how such an understanding might increase collective power for action on issues like gun violence and community safety.

When the Center for Democracy and Citizenship organized the New Citizenship project with the White House Domestic Policy Council from 1993 to 1995, analyzing the gap between citizens and government, many whom the project interviewed expressed growing distance from "citizens." As Jerome Delli Priscoli, senior policy analyst for the Institute for Water Resources in the Army Corps of Engineers, put it, "We've lost the 'civil' in civil service."[8] Paul Light, a participant in the New Citizenship project and a leading analyst of the civil service, described the ways in which government employees were once motivated by an ethos of public service that stressed their civic identities. But this ethos has largely disappeared from the civil service, replaced by a focus on specialization and service to citizens conceived as customers. "Departments and agencies have plenty of advocates for doing things for citizens and to citizens," Light observed. "But there are today almost no voices for seeing government workers as citizens themselves, working with other citizens. Citizens are viewed in partial terms— as clients and customers, taxpayers, and voters—but too rarely as whole actors, capable of judgment and problem solving."[9]

Similar patterns are present elsewhere. For instance, colleges and universities are prone to treat their students as consumers of education. Faculty interested in students as "learners" object, but do not usually stress the larger conception of citizen as co-creator. In another example, many in religious communities today decry growing materialism, but also reflect the spread of marketplace assumptions. Thus in a discussion with state legislators in 2007, Peg Chemberlin, executive director of the Minnesota Council of Churches, said that "increasingly congregants think of themselves as consumers of church, not producers of church, and congregations think of themselves as consumers of denominations, not producers of denominations. . . . In many of our denominations the trend shows up by congregations saying 'We don't like what you're doing, so we're going to quit giving you money,' which is a consumer mentality, unobligated to the denomination."[10]

Yet, despite this replacement of productive civic identities with consumer identities and the resulting erosion of the role of civic power centers in the life of communities, signs of a productive agency-based civic politics are emerging in the United States and around the world. For example, the Obama campaign of 2008, with its theme of "Yes We Can," showed possibilities for introducing civic agency on a large scale by integrating community organizing methods into its field operation. The campaign found widespread enthusiasm for the message, especially among young people. The Arab Spring generated a "sense of empowerment and civic duty," as *The Financial Times* put it.[11] In scholarly terms, signs of agency and of citizens as co-creators are illustrated by the essays in this volume.

Higher education is an "upstream" institution that shapes the citizenship identities and practices of students throughout their lives. As colleges and universities discuss and practice the civic politics of public work, they will help recreate foundations for civic agency in multiple places. There are powerful historical and cultural resources available to feed this process.

A HERITAGE OF PUBLIC WORK

A civic politics of public work, contrasted with sweeping ideological and polarizing frameworks, has rich antecedents in practical community-building efforts and also in movements that combine aspirations for substantial democratic change with a pluralist, practical, political quality.

The labor of settlers who cleared lands and who built towns and villages, wells, meeting halls, and roads generated what the historian Robert Wiebe called

America's "portable democracy."[12] Benjamin Franklin was an important philosophical architect of the concept and practice of public work. The Leather Apron Club, which he founded in Philadelphia, included tradesmen, artisans, and shopkeepers—those whom he lauded as "the middling people"—based on a vision of "doing well by doing good." Members created a street-sweeping corps, a volunteer firefighting company, a tax-supported neighborhood constabulary, health and life insurance groups, a library, a hospital, an academy for educating young people, a society for sharing scientific discoveries, and a postal system. Franklin proposed that education should combine practical and liberal arts, a union that was to reappear in the establishment of the country's land-grant colleges.[13] David Mathews described this tradition of practical community building in his treatment of the emergence of public schools and other public institutions:

> Nineteenth-century self-rule . . . was a sweaty, hands-on, problem-solving politics. The democracy of self-rule was rooted in collective decision making and acting—especially acting. Settlers on the frontier had to be producers, not just consumers. They had to join forces to build forts, roads, and libraries. They formed associations to combat alcoholism and care for the poor as well as to elect representatives. They also established the first public schools. Their efforts were examples of 'public work,' meaning work done by not just for the public.[14]

In nineteenth-century America, movements such as the first large-scale labor union organizing effort, the Knights of Labor, and populism, an interracial movement of small farmers fighting to save their land, drew on these traditions by combining visions of democratic change with more down-to-earth concerns. In addition to facilitating trade unionism, the Knights of Labor included professionals, factory workers, small business owners, and others. It focused on members' moral and political education, cooperative enterprises, and small land-holding. The Knights were able to bring together a "nostalgia for a preindustrial past, in part on a defense of devalued craft skills, but in part also on a transcendent vision of a cooperative industrial future" that also placed "imperatives toward productive work, civic responsibility, education, a wholesome family life, temperance, and self-improvement."[15]

While the Knights were largely an urban movement, populism grew out of farmers' cooperatives that spread across the South and Midwest in the 1880s. Academic critics charge that populism's idea of who makes change—"the people"—is ill-defined compared to the more rigorous definitions associated with class-based or interest-group politics. Many add that populists are *reformist*—focused on practical ends—and offer few detailed plans for breaking up concentrations of wealth and power. Yet, from a realist political vantage point—one that is skeptical about sweeping blueprints for the future or precise definitions of who should lead the process of change—these features are considerable strengths. The porousness of the concept of "the people," a narrative conception of agency, allows for inclusive definitions of peoplehood when movements seek allies and when organizers are oriented toward a diverse democracy. Similarly, populism's practicality—a "politics of getting things done," as Stephanie DeWitt put it[16]—comes from its grounding in the gritty concerns and everyday problems of living communities. Sheldon Wolin argues that populism is the "culture of democracy" itself:

> Historically [populism] has stood for the efforts of ordinary citizens and would-be citizens to survive. . . . A culture of survival is very different from a . . . market-culture littered by the disposable remains of yesterday and shaped by manipulation of attitudes and desires. . . . Its practices issued from taking care of living beings and mundane artifacts, from keeping them in the world by use and memory. To sustain the institutions of family, community, church, school and local economy demanded innovation as well as conservation. . . . The reason why democracy should be grounded in a populist culture is not because those who live it are pure, unprejudiced, and unfailingly altruistic. Rather, it is because it is a culture that . . . has learned that existence is a cooperative venture over time.[17]

A politics with some similarities to the populism of the cooperative farmers' movement, and different from defensive and parochial protest movements, emerged in the 1930s and holds lessons for us today.

As Steve Fraser has observed, one current of 1930s politics was defensive. Skilled craftsmen sometimes saw industrial unions as a threat to their identity, power, and position in the labor hierarchy. There are similarities in today's academy, where a tenured class of faculty often feel threatened by what they perceive as lower-skilled and less-experienced non-tenured and short-term faculty. Like current merit review schemes imposed on universities by state legislatures and the rush to online education by college and university administrators staffed by increasingly large numbers of non-tenured hires, craftsmen in the AFL encountered "impersonally determined and imposed piece rates, bonus systems, and job ladders, . . . [and] ingenious designs for serial production to be undertaken by a whole new class of semiskilled operatives." Like AFL craftsmen, for whom "this new industrial order promised the social extermination of a whole social species," contemporary tenured faculty, in the face of overwhelming systemic change, are sometimes paralyzed by inertia.[18]

Yet, in the 1930s, other political currents went well beyond defensive action. In the new industrial unions of the Congress of Industrial Organizations, skilled workers made common cause with semi-skilled and unskilled workers as well as with communities beyond their factories. "In the auto and electrical industries, tool and die makers and machinists comprised the indispensable cadre of the new industrial unions," according to Fraser. "Skilled workers comprised a milieu heterogeneous in background. They included both production and nonproduction workers. Some were quite secular and even anticlerical; others were attracted by liberal currents in Catholic social thought."[19]

Pluralist, coalitional politics reemerged in the civil rights movement to challenge the polarizing and righteous politics spreading among young activists. Bayard Rustin, shaped by experiences in the 1930s, was a brilliant proponent. Rustin worked for years to bring nonviolence to the freedom movement, playing a critical role in educating Martin Luther King Jr. about nonviolence during the Montgomery bus boycott. He organized the 1963 March on Washington, and was a key strategist for many other movement events. Rustin also lived a complicated life. As a gay, African American, formerly communist, nonviolent

Quaker, Rustin was extremely controversial and civil rights leaders kept him behind the scenes.

Rustin combined political realism with an expansive vision of change, and he was centrally concerned with the real work of moving from the world as it is to the world as it should be. In organizing the March on Washington, he skillfully built collaborative relationships with the White House, while keeping in mind the need for the movement to develop and advance its own independent agenda. By the mid-sixties, Rustin had become deeply worried about the growing tendency of young activists, both black and white, to substitute "posture and volume" for effective strategy.[20] His 1965 article in *Commentary* magazine, "From Protest to Politics," challenged this tendency in ways that still have relevance to the highly moralized discourses in the humanities and social sciences, and on college campuses. "Young militants," Rustin argued,

> are often described as the radicals of the movement, but they are really its moralists. They seek to change white hearts—by traumatizing them. Frequently abetted by white self-flagellants, they may gleefully applaud . . . Malcolm X because, while they admit he has no program, they think he can frighten white people into doing the right thing. But in any case, hearts are not relevant to the issue; neither racial affinities nor racial hostilities are rooted there. It is institutions—social, political, and economic institutions—which are the ultimate molders of collective sentiments. Let these institutions be reconstructed today, and let the ineluctable gradualism of history govern the formation of a new psychology.[21]

Are there contemporary examples of institutions serving as enabling environments for public work that enhances civic agency? In what follows, we present two case studies drawn from the emerging movement to revitalize the democratic purposes and practices of education.

NORTHERN ARIZONA UNIVERSITY:
REVIVING THE COLLECTIVE COMMONWEALTH[22]

For many faculty, the walls seem to be closing in. Many despair, having lost their sense of agency and any belief that they can influence the course of their institutions. Over the last several years at Northern Arizona University (NAU), a group of organizers has sought to build democratic centers of power—enabling environments—by establishing new coalitions and alliances. Key to the work have been strategies to re-empower faculty through democratic agency, to reverse the tide of faculty despair, to begin to rebuild the university as a civic institution, and to revive a cooperative spirit that is infused with a vision of the collective commonwealth of knowledge. To illustrate, we offer two examples.

In NAU's First Year Learning Initiative (FYLI), Blase Scarnati and Michelle D. Miller, a cognitive psychologist, bring faculty together to co-create new pedagogical approaches, collaborate with one another and their teaching colleagues, and build alliances around the curricular spaces they control. In addition to using other community organizing strategies, they hold one-on-one meetings off campus and build productive working relations, or "public relationships" in the language of community organizing, with course coordinators.

In these meetings, faculty members tell the narratives of their courses and the narratives of their teaching. Miller and Scarnati also explore effective pedagogies and strategies—based on their NAU experience and supported by the relevant literature—that can help students increase their learning and succeed academically. The conversations are animated by the assumptions that faculty own the curriculum and can be empowered through curricular work and that the curriculum itself can be conceived as a creative working space for innovation. Miller and Scarnati seek to use a collaborative, cooperative model for course coordination, since faculty tend to resist top-down mandates.

For many faculty, the opportunity to work cooperatively with their colleagues in order to achieve curricular ends is an invigorating—and relatively rare—experience. Many, too, are hopeful about what they can achieve in cooperation with their colleagues. Building coalitions within and among departments creates new experiences of power, while generating new and creative energies.

Most FYLI courses are multi-sectioned (the largest has seventy-five sections each term), and more than fourteen thousand students enroll in the courses each semester (not unique enrollments). Michelle Miller has compared the FYLI to more traditional redesign initiatives. For example, statewide National Center for Academic Transformation redesign initiatives conducted between 2006 and 2010 affected only fifty-five courses, with a mean of 1.45 courses per university and 9 courses per state. These courses have a broad reach across all NAU colleges and disciplines, from the biological sciences to business. Additionally, the course completion rates for students enrolled in FYLI courses increased significantly.

Through CRAFTS (Civic Engagement for Arizona Families, Transitions, and Communities), a second example of pedagogical innovation, NAU has built one of the largest programs of action research, civic agency, and public work in the country. Over three years, ninety-six percent of first-year students at NAU now enroll in FYLI courses. CRAFTS is grounded in collaboration between the Community, Culture, and Environment Program, the First Year Seminar Program, and the Masters of Arts in Sustainable Communities Program. It includes faculty from departments as diverse as education, biology, philosophy, and criminology. Each year, over 550 new first-year students join their fellow students from previous years to conduct action research in conjunction with local community organizations doing the political work to create more democratic, just, and sustainable communities.

Key to the success of CRAFTS are NAU faculty, staff, graduate assistant mentors, undergraduate peer teaching assistants, and undergraduate students. They work non-hierarchically and collectively to build new alliances with community-based partners in order to create dense rhizomatic webs of practice called Action Research Teams (ARTs). Action research begins with the organization of First Year Seminar students into course-specific working groups that feed into one of the fourteen ARTs umbrella organizations under which NAU students and faculty collaborate with members of the broader community, working on a variety of environmental, social, educational, economic, and political issues. Each ART includes a diverse mix of members: sophomores and juniors who want to continue in the public work of the ARTs and assume leadership and organizing responsibilities for initiatives within each ART; sophomore or junior peer teaching assistants from the First Year Seminar Program who work with the students in each seminar, graduate student mentors assigned to ART, and multigenerational community partners—including K-12 students and their parents, community members and organizations, and Navajo elders.

ARTs work with a variety of community organizations, such as the Coconino County Sustainable Economic Development Initiative, Friends of Flagstaff's Future, Northern Arizona Institutions for Community Leadership/Interfaith Council (Industrial Areas Foundation), and key public schools in the Flagstaff Unified School District. Many powerful stories from student and community colleagues come from ARTs work. Each semester, students organize an ARTs Symposium where working groups report on their work. Many have declared that "this work has changed my life."

Brief profiles of two of the fourteen ARTs illustrate their work. The Weatherization and Community Building Action Team (WACBAT) is a student-led effort organized around working groups in weatherization, retrofits, and community organizing. WACBAT builds community relationships and power for sustainability broadly understood, as it works to advance "green economy" initiatives designed to increase energy efficiency and promote the use of renewable energy sources. Combining research and study on these issues with door-to-door outreach and statewide organizing and advocacy, WACBAT led a campaign which successfully pressured the Arizona Corporation Commission and the local power company to establish a $2.7 million fund used to provide loans for homeowners seeking to improve energy efficiency. It has also developed many outstanding undergraduate leaders, in collaboration with a host of other community partners.

Through their civic agency and public work, the ARTs have also been effective in increasing retention among key NAU student populations. The retention rate for minority students who successfully complete First Year Seminars with ARTs (FYSeminar-ARTs) sections—those earning A, B, or C grades—is 16 percent higher than the retention rate for non-FYSeminar-ARTs minority students. The retention rate for female students who complete FYSeminar-ARTs sections is 9 percent higher than for non-FYSeminar-ARTs female students. FYSeminar-ARTs participation also significantly increases engagement with course-specific learning activities involving diversity, cultural influences, and multiple perspectives.

PUBLIC ACHIEVEMENT IN FRIDLEY MIDDLE SCHOOL[23]
At Augsburg College in Minneapolis, a group of faculty, staff, and students has been working for two years to integrate civic agency, civic politics, and public work into curricular and cocurricular experiences. The multicultural PhD program in nursing has a focus on educating "citizen nurses." The new mission statement of the education department similarly stresses the preparation of "citizen teachers" who will be innovators and leaders in shaping education. Public Achievement, a youth civic empowerment initiative, offers a striking example in Fridley Middle School, which is located in a suburban community north of Minneapolis.

Public Achievement was founded in 1990 by Harry Boyte as a contemporary version of the Citizenship Education Program (CEP), a grassroots, popular civil rights-era education initiative of the Southern Christian Leadership Conference, that had shaped him as a college student. Through CEP, African Americans and some poor whites learned skills and concepts associated with community organizing and effective change-making. CEP experiences often had dramatic impact on participants' identity, helping them see themselves not as victims, but as agents of change and civic role models for the nation.

Through participation in Public Achievement, young people learn skills, concepts, and methods of empowering public work. They work as teams guided by coaches, who may be young adults, college students, or teachers. Coaches help guide the work, but do not dominate. They also are highly attentive to the development of young people's skills and capacities for effective public work. The initiative has spread widely and is now used in schools, colleges, and communities across the United States as well as in Poland, the West Bank and Gaza, Israel, and Northern Ireland.

At Fridley Middle School, "citizen teachers" Michael Ricci and Alissa Blood have developed an empowering learning culture in special education. Students take the lead in designing their own learning, largely around self-directed public work projects of their own choosing. In the process, students who are subject to emotional and behavioral disorders and other health-related disabilities have become community leaders. "In all the other classes, the teachers tell you want to do," said one seventh grader. "In [Public Achievement], the teacher says, 'Okay, what do you want to do?'"[24]

According to *Wikipedia*, "special education" refers to "the education of students with special needs in a way that addresses the students' individual differences and needs."[25] Schools often segregate such students from the mainstream because of behaviors that interrupt the general education classroom. The problem, as the *Wikipedia* entry for "Emotional and Behavioral Disorders" (EBD) notes, is that "both general definitions as well as concrete diagnosis of EBD may be controversial as the observed behavior may depend on many factors."[26] Put differently, is the "problem" the student or the environment? According to Ricci, "The kids in our special education classroom weren't successful in mainstream classrooms, where the format has been the same for the last 100 years. The world has changed, but the classroom is pretty much the same."[27]

Susan O'Connor, director of Augsburg College's graduate program in special education, wanted to try something different. "Special education generally still uses a medical model, based on how to fix kids," she said.[28] Working with Dennis Donovan, national organizer for Public Achievement at the Center for Democracy and Citizenship, O'Connor and other faculty and graduate students at Augsburg partnered with Ricci and Blood, graduates of their program, to design an alternative. Both Ricci and Blood believed it was worth trying an approach that would give special education students the chance to take leadership in designing their own learning. "The idea of trying something different [in special education] that might give school a purpose for our kids just made sense," Blood explained, pointing out the frustration that special education students also experience.[29] Public Achievement offered resources.

In the self-contained special education classroom, where the primary concern is to teach students strategies that help them manage the disruptive behaviors that interfere with learning in school, there is latitude for innovation. "More evidence would be needed [in a mainstream classroom] to allow us to go to the level we did, where we turned Public Achievement into a core part of the curriculum," Blood said.[30]

As a result of Blood and Ricci's adaptation of Public Achievement to special education, students with challenges that would have forced their removal from conventional classrooms in many schools came to be seen as public leaders at Fridley, where they undertook projects such as rewriting district policy on school bullying, organizing a campaign for better understanding of pit bulls, creating murals to encourage healthy activities, and developing a support network for terminally ill children. Their efforts were widely recognized by the principal, teachers, and other students. They also became visible change-makers in the larger Fridley community, making presentations before school administrators, the school board, and other community leaders, and elected officials. Their work has been featured in the local paper and on Minnesota Public Radio.

The Public Achievement approach also transformed the work of Ricci and Blood. "My role [in Public Achievement] is not to fix things for the kids but to say, 'This is your class, your mission. How are you going to do the work?' Our main task is to remind them, to guide them, not to tell them what to do," Ricci explained.[31] The teachers became partners with their students, who, in turn, chose the issues and learned how to address them effectively.

The students' public work created multiple opportunities for them to develop academically, because Ricci and Blood were highly intentional about making the connections. As part of the projects mentioned above, for example, students composed well-written letters seeking permission from the principal for a project, and they used math to figure out how to scale their murals in order to determine how much wall space would be needed. The focus of the teachers also changed, from "teaching to the test" to working alongside young people as they develop agency. Ricci and Blood's curriculum builds skills and habits of citizenship, such as negotiation, compromise, initiative, planning, organizing, and public speaking. It also develops what Blood called "a public professional persona."[32] Both teachers are convinced that these skills and habits will serve the students well throughout their lives.

Michael Ricci and Alissa Blood are developing a new model of the "citizen teacher" according to which the teacher is not the object of educational reform, but rather the agent and architect of reform. In an environment where teachers and faculty across the country feel powerless, they serve as powerful role models for educators moving into a proactive stance.

CONCLUSION

At every level, educational institutions have enormous power that operates invisibly to shape identities, assumptions, and ways of looking at the world. Higher education, in particular, creates credentialed knowledge of many kinds, including pedagogical approaches in K-12 schooling. Colleges and universities generate and diffuse conceptual frameworks that structure work practices. They socialize professionals and also convey meanings of citizenship. They are resources for economic and community vitality. In light of such powers, colleges and universities can be seen as *anchoring institutions of citizenship*.

Efforts to renew the democratic purposes of higher education are part of a larger context, what can be seen as an emerging movement for citizen empowerment and citizen-centered democracy. It is important to integrate the several strands of this movement in a new public narrative in which the great majority of people can see their interests and aspirations reflected. These strands include organizing on questions of poverty and inequality, efforts to address climate change, and institutional change experiments in which professionals see themselves as *citizens* working with fellow citizens.

We are on the cusp of a new stage in this movement, which can create solid foundations for the aspirations to civic agency that are exploding across the world. In this time of dramatic change in the educational landscape, some colleges and universities will move to its forefront and play key roles. They will be "democracy's colleges" of the twenty-first century.

NOTES

1. Harry Boyte, Stephen Elkin, Peter Levine, Jane Mansbridge, Elinor Ostrom, Karol Sołtan, and Rogers Smith, "The New Civic Politics: Civic Theory and Practice for the Future," framing statement of the Summer Institute of Civic Studies, September 28, 2007, http://activecitizen .tufts.edu/circle/summer-institute/summer-institute-of-civic-studies-framing-statement.
2. Scobey, "Why Now? Because This Is a Copernican Moment," in *Civic Provocations*, ed. Donald W. Harward (Washington, DC: Bringing Theory to Practice, 2012), 3–4.
3. For further discussion of "world building," see Arendt, *The Human Condition* (Chicago: University of Chicago Press, 1958), 136–58.
4. As Aristotle put it in *The Politics*, "The nature of the *polis* is to be a plurality . . . made up not only of so many men but of different kinds of men." *The Politics*, ed. Stephen Everson (New York: Cambridge University Press, 1966), 31. For an extended discussion of the ways contemporary politics has eroded the understanding of politics as engaged plurality, see Harry Chatten Boyte, "A different Kind of Politics: John Dewey and the Meaning of Citizenship in the 21st Century," *The Good Society* 12, no. 2 (2003): 1–15.
5. Galston, "Realism in Political Theory," *European Journal of Political Theory* 9, no. 4 (2011): 385–86.
6. Honig, *Political Theory and the Displacement of Politics* (Ithaca: Cornell University Press, 1993) 2.
7. Elkin, *Reconstructing the Commercial Republic: Constitutional Design after Madison* (Chicago: University of Chicago Press, 2006), 257.
8. Boyte coordinated the New Citizenship; Carmen Sirianni, research director, interviewed dozens of federal employees. See Carmen Sirianni and Lewis Friedland, *Civic Innovation in America: Community Empowerment, Public Policy, and the Movement for Civic Renewal* (Berkeley: University of California, 2001); and Harry Boyte and Nan Kari, *Building America: The Democratic Promise of Public Work* (Philadelphia: Temple University Press, 1996). Delli Priscoli quoted in *Building America,* 198.
9. Light, discussion with Boyte, May 1995.
10. Chamberlin, prepared remarks, public forum on citizenship with state legislators, May 11, 2006, Minnesota State Capitol, St. Paul, organized by the Center for Democracy and Citizenship.
11. Borzou Daragahi, "Cairo's Voters Shrug at Poll Upheaval," *Financial Times,* April 20, 2012. Daragahi also reports on the subsequent fading of the "sense of empowerment and civic duty" that resulted from the Arab Spring—evident long before the bitter clashes between the Marsi government and its opponents.

12. Robert Wiebe, *Self-Rule: A Cultural History of American Democracy* (Chicago: University of Chicago Press, 1995).

13. Walter Isaacson, "The American Ben Franklin Saw," *Washington Post*, November 21, 2012.

14. Mathews, *Reclaiming Public Education by Reclaiming Our Democracy* (Dayton, OH: Kettering Foundation Press, 2006), vii.

15. Leon Fink, *Workingmen's Democracy: The Knights of Labor and American Politics* (Chicago: University of Illinois Press, 1983), 8–12.

16. DeWitt, "Reflections on Populism," (unpublished manuscript in Boyte's possession, November 28, 2006).

17. Wolin, "Contract and Birthright," in *The New Populism: The Politics of Empowerment,* ed. Harry C. Boyte and Frank Riessman (Philadelphia: Temple University Press), 285–6.

18. Fraser, "The 'Labor Question,'" in *The Rise and Fall of the New Deal Order, 1930–1980,* ed. Steve Fraser and Gary Gerstle (Princeton, NJ: Princeton University Press, 1989), 63.

19. Ibid, 65.

20. Rustin, "From Protest to Politics: The Future of the Civil Rights Movement," in *Negro Protest Thought in the Twentieth Century*, ed. Francis L. Broderick and August Meier (New York: Bobbs-Merrill, 1965), 414.

21. Ibid., 413.

22. The section on Northern Arizona University is written by Blase Scarnati.

23. This section on Fridley Public Achievement was written by Harry Boyte and Jennifer Nelson, a graduate student in public policy at the Humphrey School of Public Affairs.

24. "Public Achievement in Fridley—Transforming Special Education," YouTube video, 38:27, posted by "publicworkcitizen," June 2, 2013, www.youtube.com/watch?v=VaRimtavig8.

25. "Special Education," *Wikipedia*, last modified October 10, 2013, http://en.wikipedia.org/wiki/Special_education.

26. "Emotional and Behavioral Disorders," *Wikipedia*, last modified October 3, 2013, http://en.wikipedia.org/wiki/Emotional_and_behavioral_disorders.

27. Michael Rissi and Alissa Blood, interview by Jennifer Nelson, March 12, 2013.

28. "Public Achievement in Fridley," YouTube Video.

29. See note 27.

30. Ibid.

31. Ibid.

32. Ibid.

Citizen-Centered Research for Civic Studies: Bottom Up, Problem Driven, Mixed Methods, Interdisciplinary

8

Sanford F. Schram

ONE WAY TO CONCEIVE OF CIVIC STUDIES is to see it as an emerging field, not yet a full-fledged discipline of the contemporary academy. Yet, we can trace a prehistory over the centuries—back even to the ancient Greeks, Plato and Aristotle included—for what is at the heart of the developing field of civic studies is actually the longstanding dream to marry theory and practice so that political thought can better inform public action. A significant thread of the Western tradition is a conversation about how truth can speak to power, how theory can inform practice, how citizens can be educated to be self-governing. In fact, as democratic aspirations continue to spread around the globe, the orientation underlying much research and writing is increasingly focused not just on integrating knowledge and power, or theory and practice, but also about how a theoretically-informed practice can be politically efficacious, not only for political elites and others who dominate public deliberations and the policymaking process, but for ordinary citizens with their own aspirations for participating in systems of democratic governance.

In what follows, I want to make a point of emphasis: contemporary social science research can play an important role in helping make civic studies relevant to collective action in the public sphere today, and it can best do that when it is focused on helping citizens be able to better participate in public deliberation. Specifically, I want to argue for a citizen-centered research that can help make civic studies a more democratically empowering enterprise. My thesis is that a civic studies informed by citizen-centered research can help reorient the study of public affairs so as to enhance the participation of citizens in their own democracies. The focus of such research would be on citizens as subjects for action, rather than as objects of inquiry. The goal would be not to know what is true about democratic citizens merely as empirical fact, but instead to foster research that is consciously designed to produce information that can develop insights into how citizens can be better empowered as self-determining agents in their own democratic deliberations. A civic studies grounded in this type of citizen-centered research would, therefore, be designed to put knowledge of democracy in the hands of the people who make that democracy come alive in practice. Reconceived in this way, civic studies would connect theory and practice so as actually to strengthen both, especially in their relationship to enhancing democracy, thereby making practice more reflexive while making theory more self-consciously reflective of the real challenges of practicing democracy. The relays between theories of democracy and the practical challenges of democracy would serve as circuits for recharging both the theory and practice of democracy, even as they are revised in the process.

Given my emphasis on research, I think it is particularly important to highlight the ways in which research would change once incorporated into a civic studies that has been revised to have a citizen-centered focus. The practice of research would be very different from the way it is normally practiced today in the various social science disciplines. First, civic studies research would start from the premise that it is all about growing and reflecting ties to democratic practice, with a specific orientation to enhancing the capacity of ordinary citizens to participate more effectively in public decision-making processes at all stages of public policy making: defining problems, setting agendas, designing policy, legislating, implementing and evaluating public policies. Empirical investigation of democratic challenges would, under these circumstances, morph from the abstract study of generalizations about democratic participation into a tool for citizens to better address the real, specific, concrete challenges they confront in the process of collective decision making and problem solving.

Citizen-centered research for civic studies would, by definition, have to be conducted from the bottom up, looking at problems from the perspectives of democratic citizens, rather than from the top down, from the perspective of the state. It would also be explicitly problem driven, addressing real problems in specific contexts as democratic citizens confront them, rather than seeking to understand democratic processes in the abstract, as in the case of theory-driven or method-driven research. Such bottom-up, problem-driven research would not be tied to a particular methodological orientation; it would mix methods of empirical investigation as necessary to better understand specific problems, rather than focus on perfecting a particular method or technique of analysis or investigation. It also would be interdisciplinary, foregoing the building of knowledge in a particular discipline for the sake of enhancing the ability of real citizens to address concrete democratic challenges in specific contexts.

This chapter specifies the role of citizen-centered research for civic studies, its general contours and characteristics, challenges to its practice both within and outside the academy, and its contributions to the bridging of democratic theory and practice. The chapter provides examples of work already being conducted that can be said to be consistent with my vision of citizen-centered research for civic studies. In particular, this chapter highlights the "practical turn" in social science, especially as represented by Bent Flyvbjerg's call for a phronetic social science,[1] as an example of the type of research that is well suited to enhancing knowledge for a citizen-centered civic studies.

RETHINKING RESEARCH FOR CIVIC STUDIES

Just as civic studies needs to be oriented toward a citizen-centered perspective, so too does social science research, especially if it is going to better serve a civic studies that is focused on empowering ordinary citizens to be more effective participants in their own democratic deliberations. When we think about what has long been called the "conduct of inquiry," we often think about methodology and assume that methodology involves the collection of data for purposes of making objective, fact-based claims about empirical reality. Yet, this is too hasty an assumption, for it moves right past a prior question: what is the perspective from which the researcher comes to view the data being collected? This optical issue is fundamental, for it enables us to question the false objectivity that comes with pretending that our view as researchers is but a "view from nowhere."[2] This is the core critical conceit of what we can call "scientistic social science," which is grounded in the belief that social science research can and should be impartial, unbiased, and therefore objective in offering a view of its subject matter so as, in turn, to offer an accurate representation of the empirical facts of what is being studied. A more robust objectivity, however, would make explicit that each and every research investigation is conducted from a specific perspective or angle of vision that should be accounted for in interpreting its presentation of what it is offering as fact.

The major social science disciplines, however, still tend to be organized around an ivory tower model of research. The center of gravity in each of the social science disciplines—whether it is sociology, political science, economics, geography and related fields—still is heavily tilted toward the ideal that the best research is politically neutral so as to claim it is unbiased. Yet, even politically neutral research is still grounded in a particular perspective that biases what it sees and how. The idealized version of social science research also tends to hew to the related orientation that its goal should be to study the social world in a scientific fashion in the sense of producing objective understandings based on testing hypotheses that demonstrate the viability of causal laws for explaining social phenomena. This orientation reflects the pervasive influence of the belief that the natural sciences represent the paragon of scientific investigation and that all other fields of inquiry that aspire to be scientific need to emulate them. Yet, the aping of the natural sciences by the social sciences inevitably ends up overstressing the pursuit of knowledge of universal rationality at the expense of situated reasoning as to what is rational in particular circumstances. What is, in fact, sacrificed in this case is the effort to produce knowledge that can help inform actors about how to act in specific situations, something a citizen-centered civic studies is all about. To the extent that conventional social science persists in this scientistic orientation focused on emulating the natural sciences' quest for generalizable causal laws to explain what is studied, it is therefore a disabling practice of less than helpful relevance to a civic studies that itself grows out of the concerns of ordinary citizens and seeks to help inform and empower their efforts to address particular problems they are confronting as democratic actors.

Once we give up the lie of a "view from nowhere" and account for perspective, it turns out that there is reason to be concerned about much of mainstream social science, especially political science, and the implications for its relevance to civic studies. For too long, political science and related disciplines, when they have been turned to emphasizing their relevance to taking action in the public arena, have been focused on understanding the realm of civic action from a top-down perspective designed to enhance the capacity of political elites and policy makers. A top-down perspective orients the researcher, consciously or not, toward seeing what is being studied as a problem to be managed. Conventional political science research often falls into this trap. While often criticized for being disconnected, abstract, and in quest of universal generalizations, conventional research tends, at least implicitly, to reflect a top-down perspective that actually motivates a kind of technicism whereby research ends up in service of the management of a problem, whether it is the micro-level issue of low information among potential voters, for example, or the macro-level issue of the causes of war.

Once we see that the conventional approach to political research is not without perspective, that it does not reflect the "view from nowhere," but in fact that it is reflective of a distinctive perspective that implies a certain orientation toward acting in the world, then we can begin to become interested in posing alternative perspectives. The goal is not to realize the impossible dream of getting beyond perspective, but rather to embrace a more robust objectivity that is based on the idea that a researcher consciously chooses a perspective and explicitly defends it as a useful orientation for informing and motivating a more defensible politics. For those researchers interested in having their research enhance the capacity of ordinary citizens to participate more effectively in democratic deliberation regarding specific challenges and problems they confront, adopting a bottom-up perspective follows logically. Disciplined research conducted from the bottom-up and designed to enhance the capacities of ordinary people to wield power in the policy process has been in short supply. Calls for a public sociology in recent years are emblematic of the winds of change that are sweeping across the social sciences in that they not only highlight a desire for relevance to the realm of public action, but also make that relevance primarily about empowering people on the bottom of the structure of power.

In the area of public policy, a researcher who takes a bottom-up approach studies a policy from the perspective of the people most directly affected by the implementation of that policy. To emphasize a bottom-up perspective for research geared to contributing to a citizen-centered civic studies is not to suggest that it should be the only, or definitive, perspective taken in such research; rather, it is to recognize that this perspective—woefully underutilized today—is an important, even critical, alternative. Bringing a bottom-up perspective into research for civic studies is particularly needed in studies of public policy, which still to this day all too often continue to be premised on a top-down perspective that focuses on issues of concern to the people tasked with managing the implementation of policies. A good corrective would be to counter these top-down studies with research framed by a bottom-up perspective, one that focuses on how the clients, the recipients, the taxpayers, the regulated, and others experience the implementation of a particular public policy as they encounter it through their interactions with the agencies and officials who administer the program in question. Here we get to see not just the formal policy, but the operant policy in terms of its effects on ordinary people.

A most articulate call for such citizen-centered, bottom-up research is provided by Nancy Naples, who called for what she labels an "everyday world policy analysis" that examines policy by acquiring information for the people most directly affected by it so as to highlight what the policy means to them.[3] My research with Corey Shdaimah and Roland Stahl, conducted on behalf of the Affordable Housing Coalition in Philadelphia in order to get the Philadelphia Housing Trust Fund created, was grounded in Naples's perspective.[4] Naples's insistence on looking at policy from the perspective of those most directly affected by it inspired us to study and then describe low-income housing policies in Philadelphia by undergoing the process by which low-income applicants applied for and received housing assistance of various kinds. We found that the actual experience was quite different from the ways these policies are described. We found that long waiting times, for instance, made the limited assistance to be received, as in the case of home repair programs or loans for home purchases, less likely to reach all the people who were interested in receiving assistance and less effective when it did reach applicants who waited out the process.

Everyday world policy analysis is an example of bottom-up research that helps shine a democratizing light on public policies. It produces research that is not only informed by a client perspective, but that also helps empower clients to add the substance of empirical research to their plaintive pleas for redress of their public policy grievances. It is research that grows out of citizen concerns and feeds back into efforts to have those concerns taken seriously by policy makers. It is citizen-centered research for a civic studies that can help empower ordinary people to be more effective participants in their own democracy.

But citizen-centered research for civic studies should be more than just bottom up in its perspective. It should also be problem driven. Conventional social science, mortgaged as it is to the naturalistic model of inquiry, is premised on the idea of testing theories in order to confirm or reject hypotheses about causal relationships. The goal is to produce generalizations about what causes what to happen in the social world. As a result, this research tends to be what we can call "theory driven"; that is, the theories about causal relationships are the fundamental premise for the research. The animating purpose of such research is, therefore, to serve theory by advancing the project of providing theoretical explanations for how things are caused to happen in any one field of inquiry. Yet, improving theory in the quest of producing durable generalizations about social phenomena is of questionable value for a social world where actors have the consciousness and reflexive capabilities to internalize explanations and choose to respond to them. Understanding, predicting, and explaining the actions of the actors being studied becomes all the more elusive under these conditions.

By contrast, citizen-centered research for civic studies is premised on the idea that, instead of being treated as objects of inquiry, these actors should be empowered as subjects who can better choose how to act on the basis of research into the issues, problems, and challenges they are confronting. I would like to suggest that the object-subject inversion here lies at the heart of switching from "theory-driven" to "problem-driven" research. The ontological shift away from seeing the social world as caused by exogenous factors and toward viewing the social world as a field that conscious actors choose how to negotiate moves us, even motivates us, as researchers, to reorient our inquiries away from studying social actors as objects to be explained to seeing them as subjects to be empowered—hopefully, in part, by our research. This refocusing moves research away from trying to develop more and better generalizable theory to trying to find out what are the problems that confront actors and then researching those problems in service of helping those actors better address them. The shift from theory-driven to problem-driven research is, therefore, a shift away from trying to understand what is generalizable to focusing on what can be done to address problems in specific, situated, localized contexts (at whatever level, be it local, state, or national). This shift is in service of helping empower people in particular situated contexts better confront the challenges that are inhibiting them from becoming more effective participants in their own democracy. In other words, seen in this way, a bottom-up perspective and problem-driven research go together.

Once we embrace the idea of taking a problem-driven approach to our bottom-up investigations of the challenges confronting ordinary people who are seeking to be more effective democratic participants, we become less wedded to a particular type of analysis, quantitative or qualitative, and more open to mixing different methodological orientations and methods of data collection— all in service of enhancing the ability of the people we are studying to become better democratic participants. Yet, it has not been easy getting to the point at which we can deemphasize the importance of methods in the name of enhancing our ability as researchers to use whatever methods, separately or in combination, so as to more fully and better understand specific problems confronting ordinary people in situated contexts. The current debate about methodological pluralism has been a long time coming, arriving at the end of an arduous journey across the methodological minefields that have wracked the social sciences, political science in particular. The pressures for a unitary paradigm have amounted to a real and persistent temptation—and not just for those researchers wedded to the naturalistic model.

Part of the explanation is that there are understandable reasons to insist on methodological purity as opposed to what is now being called "methodological pluralism."[5] Each social science is an academic discipline; and as with all academic disciplines, each is organized to promote scholarship according to the highest standards of what counts as good research in that discipline. In fact, we could say that the temptation to "discipline research" is therefore implicit in the very idea of organizing an academic discipline. Gatekeeping to keep out bad research and include only good research is an unavoidable corollary and ultimately leads to a preoccupation with method.

The hegemony of the "scientistic" paradigm has prevailed throughout much of the history of the social sciences, from their inception in the latter part of the nineteenth century through today. It often went under the banner of "positivism" (from the mid-nineteenth-century social theorist Auguste Comte, but also from the philosophy of science labeled "logical positivism" that was promoted by Carl Hempel and other influential thinkers associated with the Vienna Circle in the early twentieth century). While the push for a unitary discipline that insisted on a methodological purity founded on positivism could be countered with a call for a methodological pluralism, the most common response until most recently has been to push for a more "interpretive" approach to the study of politics instead. The interpretive approach is really a loose collection of many different approaches, including political ethnography, constructivism, discourse analysis, thick description, narrative analysis, and many others. What these approaches share in common is an emphasis on the interpretive dimensions of political analysis, one that stresses the importance of accounting for how political phenomena, relationships, and processes are not so much preexisting objective facts of the social world as they are subjectively experienced and interpreted phenomena. This distinction revisits the debates that preoccupied Max Weber and his colleagues at the turn of the twentieth century over whether the fledgling social sciences ought to be more about *erklaren* (explanation) or *verstehen* (understanding). Interpretive approaches emphasize that it is more important to try to arrive at an understanding of how the social world is subjectively experienced and interpreted by people than it is to provide an explanation of what causes social phenomena to happen. Most interpretive approaches, therefore, do not look to the natural sciences for a model of how to conduct research on politics, because they see an asymmetry between the social sciences and the natural sciences stemming from what Anthony Giddens and others have called the "double hermeneutic."[6] From this perspective, even the natural sciences are interpretive in that natural science research is framed through interpretive lenses for constructing the facts that are observed, whether they be quarks within atoms or black holes in the cosmology; however, the social sciences are doubly hermeneutical in that research on social phenomena involves interpreting the interpretations social actors make of their experiences. Social science research is doubly hermeneutical because it involves researchers' interpretations of other people's interpretations.

The "interpretive turn," as it came to be called in the social sciences, had many sources, including, perhaps most prominently, Clifford Geertz and his leadership in the School of Social Science at the Institute for Advanced Study in Princeton, New Jersey. Geertz, to be sure, saw interpretive approaches as providing important perspectives for understanding whatever was being studied, and he famously argued that thick description comprised "piled up inferences and implication."[7] Yet, Geertz resisted the idea that researchers had to choose either an interpretive or positivist approach as a distinct logic of inquiry. Nonetheless, over time, the main thrust of the interpretive turn has been to insist that the notion of an interpretive social science implied a distinct logic of inquiry that prevented mixing methodologies.

Positivism and interpretivism became the oil and water of political science research. While researchers might be able to mix different methods of data collection, they increasingly were discouraged from mixing methodologies on the grounds that positivism and interpretivism implied distinct logics of inquiry that could not be sensibly combined in the same analysis. Over time, this separate logic of inquiry argument has undoubtedly contributed to the idea that political science is a fractured discipline where different researchers employing different approaches talk less and less to each other.

Yet, in recent years, the longstanding impasse between positivism and inter-pretivism has begun to be undone by researchers who pursue more problem-driven, mixed-methods research. Mixed-methods research, in particular, has attracted a growing number of proponents in political science as well as in other social sciences. There are books and whole journals dedicated to promoting the idea of mixing methods in the name of engaging in problem-driven research. The idea of mixed-methods research itself can be contained within either the positivist or interpretivist paradigm, and one can find different versions of it in different instances in the social sciences. As the popularity of mixed-methods research continues to grow, so too does the possibility for more problem-driven research, including problem-driven research conducted from the bottom-up. As a result, the changing environment within disciplines becomes more hospitable for research that can contribute to a citizen-centered civic studies.

Actually, by the time we reach this stage, we can begin to see how the changing environment is opening more possibilities for moving beyond the disciplinary limits of the conventional social sciences and embracing interdisciplinary research. And once beyond the limits of the disciplines and their theoretical and methodological preoccupations, researchers are freed up to conduct research designed to contribute to a citizen-centered civic studies—that is, research that can focus on the challenges ordinary people are confronting as democratic actors. Or, at least, so we can hope.

PHRONETIC SOCIAL SCIENCE AND CIVIC STUDIES

Not a moment too soon, it seems in recent years, there is a growing interest in taking yet another turn beyond the interpretive turn, the discursive turn and still other turns—this time one that can help underwrite a meaningful role for social science research in a citizen-centered civic studies. Flora Cornish (2012) has labeled it the "practical turn,"[8] by which she is referencing the work of Bent Flyvbjerg and others who are following in his call for a revised approach to social science much along the lines I have specified in the preceding section. As with any movement, sometimes the agenda can be pushed too far—in this case, by suggesting that all research should have immediate practical relevance, eschewing the use of abstract theories that are not immediately digestible by public policy makers, or should be in service of the state. Yet, many social scientists of various stripes, from empirical researchers to theorists, have warmed to the idea that more effort should be made to connect the disciplines to ongoing political struggles. Moreover, at least in the context of the United Kingdom, government assessment of political science research output now includes significant attention to the impact of research on practice, which creates new incentives for problem-based research of the kind I advocate here.

Flyvbjerg calls his approach "phronetic social science." Phronetic social science promotes mixed-methods, problem-driven, contextualized studies that relate to specific issues political communities are struggling to address. In his 2001 book, *Making Social Science Matter*, Flyvbjerg eloquently describes the two main complaints about the social sciences, dominated as they are by the positivistic paradigm: (1) mainstream research too often mistakenly seeks to apply the methods of the natural sciences to the study of social phenomena; and (2) as a result, research too often is disconnected from any attempt to help people address the problems they are confronting. Without the labels, Flyvbjerg called for problem-driven, mixed-methods research that offers contextually specific understandings of social problems in ways that help the people being studied to better address their problems.

It was by drawing on the Aristotelian categorization of types of knowledge that Flyvbjerg called his approach "phronetic social science." For Aristotle, *episteme* was universal knowledge, *techné* was essentially the practical application of that knowledge in the form a technique, and *phronesis* was the practical wisdom that emerged from having an intimate familiarity with what works in particular settings and circumstances. For Flyvbjerg, while the natural sciences studied a subject matter of the physical world that was amenable to universal models of causal laws and such, the social sciences could not produce such knowledge of the social world given their subject matter, namely, people whose subjective states of consciousness and shared understandings are not amenable to being modeled by transcontextual, universal, causal models. Instead, Flyvbjerg said the social sciences were better adapted to provide contextually specific knowledge that could help people address the major problems they confront in their lives. Social science could conduct research that would enhance phronesis, the practical wisdom born of an intimate familiarity with a practice that could help people act effectively in particular situations. Cornish notes that

> phronesis can be understood as part of a "turn to practice" in the social sciences. After the "linguistic" and "cultural" turns gave center-stage to symbols and meanings in human affairs, attention to practice is one way of returning materiality to social theory. Phronetic social researchers engage in detail in the complexities of the phenomena which they study, examining why things are the way they are, often uncovering undesirable workings of power, and asking how things could be improved. In so doing, they develop both practical wisdom and theoretical tools that provide lenses for problematizing and reconstructing practices in other settings. They explicitly do not strive to create general or universal theories of human behavior.[9]

Flyvbjerg has argued that there is nothing new in linking political science with phronesis, and his argument highlights how a phronetic political science (and, by implication, phronetic social science more generally) are actually forms of civic studies along the lines I have been suggesting in this chapter. Flyvbjerg has noted that Aristotle explicitly linked political science and phronesis in the *Nicomachean Ethics*, which today is still foundational in studies of phronesis. Aristotle emphasized that "political science and prudence [*phronesis*] are the same state of mind" and that political science must deal both with general legislation and particular circumstances and must be practical and deliberative. "Prudence [*phronesis*] concerning the state [the object of political science, for Aristotle] has two aspects: one, which is controlling and directive, is legislative science; the other . . . deals with particular circumstances . . . [and] is practical and deliberative."[10]

Two things are worth noting here. First is Aristotle's assertion that political science—as a consequence of the emphasis on the particular, on context, and

on experience—cannot be practiced as *episteme*. To be a knowledgeable researcher in an epistemic sense is not enough when it comes to political science
because "although [people] develop ability in geometry and mathematics and
become wise in such matters, they are not thought to develop prudence [*phronesis*],"
according to Aristotle. A well-functioning political science based on *phronesis* is
imperative for a well-functioning society, says Aristotle, inasmuch as "it is impossible to secure one's own good independently of . . . political science."[11] Second,
we may benefit from paying close attention to Aristotle's emphases in his concept of phronetic political science of both the collective (the state) and the particular, of control and circumstance, of directives and deliberation, of sovereign
power and individual power.

Flyvbjerg noted that since the time of Aristotle, an unfortunate division has
developed in political philosophy of two separate traditions, each representing
one of the two sides stressed by Aristotle.[12] One tradition, the dominant one, has
developed from Plato via Hobbes and Kant to Habermas and other rationalist
thinkers, emphasizing the first of the two sides. The other, Aristotelian in origin,
has developed via Machiavelli to Nietzsche—and to Foucault, in some interpretations. Today, Flyvbjerg noted, the two traditions tend to live separate lives, apart
from occasional attacks from thinkers within one tradition on thinkers within
the other—the critique by Habermas of Foucault and Derrida, and vice versa,
being cases in point. Yet, Flyvbjerg emphasized that Aristotle wisely insisted that
what is interesting, for understanding and for praxis, is what happens where the
two now largely separate intellectual traditions intersect—where particular
circumstance and context meet general rules of governance and conduct—and
that this point of intersection is the locus of appropriate phronetic activity.[13]

Flyvbjerg's call for a phronetic social science reconnects these competing
philosophical traditions, laying the basis for a more politically engaged approach
to research that is focused on the role of power in addressing specific public issues.
In recent years, his work has been joined by a growing number of researchers
who want to connect their work to people's efforts to address public problems and
make change in the political arena. There is now a growing interest in following
Flyvbjerg by pursuing problem-driven, mixed-method research in the social
sciences today. It is not difficult to see how research into the politics of health
care, climate change, airport expansions, human rights, transitional justice,
urban planning, poverty alleviation, conflict, and other topics would benefit
from the application of the phronetic approach. The knowledge community
around these and other significant issues is replete with the "unconsciously
competent" expertise that ought to be part of the scholarly endeavor. Well-designed
problem-driven research that is informed by this knowledge community and
fortified by systematic research analysis challenges many of the dominant understandings, framings, and hegemonic discourses of these issues as well as the
relations of power that sustain them.

The phronetic approach focuses specifically on the role of power in public
problem solving. In *Real Social Science*, the volume I coedited with Flyvbjerg
and Todd Landman, we identified a remarkable set of common "tension points"
across eight case studies that form the core of the book. Whether analyzing

Native American people in Canada, women reentering the workforce in New York, or the New Labour government in the United Kingdom pursuing a policy of "sustainable aviation," the idea of "tension points" emerged as a critical theme across the case studies. Such tension points consist of "power relations that are particularly susceptible to *problematization* and thus *change*, because they are fraught with *dubious practices, contestable knowledge,* and potential *conflict*."[14] In fact, the identification and investigation of these tension points, across whatever area of policy, can bring about significant change, as these points are analogous to the tiny exploitable fissures in a rock face that, when hit often enough with a hammer, can bring down a mountainside. For us, tension points are "the fault lines phronetic researchers seek out"[15] In other words, the tension points identified through phronetic research go to the heart of political analysis. Indeed, our own research on megaprojects (Flyvbjerg), human rights (Landman), and poverty and race (Schram) use social scientific analysis to challenge power relations and bring about positive social change by focusing on tension points. In this way, we are engaged in value-based, problem-driven research that in many ways sidesteps the whole problem of positivism versus interpretivism.

Challenging power relations by doing phronetic political science focused on tension points can be a conflictual and, in some instances, adversarial process. This is particularly the case as scholars insert their research into the breaches they are studying in order to affect change. People who stand to win from the change may applaud the research, but people who stand to lose are likely to oppose it. Tension points "bite back." If nobody cares about your research, positively or negatively, perhaps it is time to reconsider its relevance. For some researchers, and perhaps especially early-career scholars and graduate students, the level of public attention and conflict that may ensue when tension points bite back can possibly be intimidating.

IT IS NOW TIME FOR A CITIZEN-CENTERED CIVIC STUDIES

The advent of phronetic social science is indicative of a healthy ferment in the social sciences, one that connects well with a citizen-centered civic studies. More research is being produced that takes a bottom-up, problem-driven, mixed-methods, interdisciplinary approach. This research is often focused on helping ordinary people in situated contexts confront challenges to their being more effective participants in their own democracy. As a result, opportunities are growing for social scientists to make a difference to the communities and societies in which they live and work. Political science, in particular, stands to benefit from these developments. Political science was founded as a discipline dedicated to fusing science and democracy. From this perspective, political science has always been, first and foremost, about political practice; its efforts to understand politics have always focused on helping improve political practice, and the expectation has been that the empirical research political scientists engage in ought to do so as well.

More research is being produced that takes a bottom-up, problem-driven, mixed-methods, interdisciplinary approach

Today, there is ferment in the social sciences that is pushing past method-ological debates, encouraging a mixing of methods in order to better connect political science research to political practice. Phronetic social science can contribute to this ferment. It provides a thoughtful approach to better connect political science research to ongoing political struggle. Like phronetic researchers in other fields, phronetic political scientists do not hide in the ivory tower of academia; they have the courage and skills to enter into the fray of public debate and policy with their research. They know that knowledge is power and that they have a civic duty to use this power—and to use it wisely, that is, phronetically—in the service of the communities in which they live. In the process, they can help catalyze a meaningful role for social science research in a citizen-centered civic studies—something that, if you think about it, is at the heart of what political science has always been about.

NOTES

1. See Flyvbjerg, *Making Social Science Matter: Why Social Inquiry Fails and How It Can Succeed Again* (New York: Cambridge University Press, 2001).
2. See Thomas Nagel, *The View from Nowhere* (New York: Oxford University Press, 1989).
3. Nancy Naples, *Feminism and Method: Ethnography, Discourse Analysis, and Activist Research* (New York: Routledge, 2003).
4. Shdaimah, Stahl, and Schram, *Change Research: A Case Study on Collaborative Methods for Social Workers and Advocates* (New York: Columbia University Press, 2011).
5. See John Dryzek, "A Pox on Perestroika, a Hex on Hegemony: Toward a Critical Political Science," in *Perestroika! The Raucous Rebellion in Political Science*, ed. Kristen Renwick Monroe (New Haven: Yale University Press, 2005), 509–25.
6. Giddens, *New Rules of Sociological Method: A Positive Critique of Interpretative Sociologies* (London: Hutchinson, 1976).
7. Geertz, *The Interpretation of Cultures* (New York: Basic Books, 1977), 7.
8. Cornish, "Book Review, *Real Social Science: Applied Phronesis*," *LSE Review of Books* (blog), Sept. 6, 2012.
9. Ibid.
10. Aristotle, *The Nicomachean Ethics*, trans. J.A.K. Thomson, revised with notes and appendices by Hugh Tredennick, introduction and bibliography by Jonathan Barnes (Harmondsworth, UK: Penguin, 1976), 1141b8–b27.
11. Ibid.
12. Flyvbjerg, *Making Social Science Matter*, 110–12.
13. Ibid.
14. Flyvbjerg, Landman, and Schram, *Real Social Science: Applied Phronesis* (New York: Cambridge University Press, 2012), 288.
15. Ibid., 290.

Public Sociology, Engaged Research, and Civic Education

9

Philip Nyden

THE DEVELOPMENT of more community-engaged forms of public sociology and the broader use of collaborative research represent bridges to, or building blocks for, civic studies. In some of its iterations, the newly framed "public sociology" is creating a new orientation to research that is expanding sociology's theoretical and methodological view about who produces knowledge. The "public" can refer to policy makers and other public audiences of experts and professionals outside of academia who might use sociological research. It can also refer to a broader "public" of everyday citizens and community members who are rarely considered consumers of sociological research. More importantly, public sociology is opening the door to citizens as co-researchers. It is opening the door to a view that citizens are creative agents and can be "co-creators" of knowledge. While one goal of public sociology is merely to get sociological research into the hands of policy makers and more users among organizations and interest groups outside of academia, another goal is to institutionalize a new organic form of public sociology that brings non-sociologists and broader groups of citizens into the research process as equal partners. This new emphasis creates a logical bridge to civic studies.

The discussion presented in this chapter is informed, in part, by the author's experience as co-chair of the American Sociological Association (ASA) Task Force on Public Sociology as well as his leadership role in the ASA Section on Sociological Practice and Public Sociology. Both the task force and the section have been at the center of discussions about better connecting sociology to a broader range of consumers and about collaborative research methods that involve broader publics in defining and completing research projects.

Independent of the growth of public sociology is an increase in the use of collaborative researcher-practitioner research models. These models operate in settings where community partners work directly with university researchers to conduct research that informs the direction of civil society by directly linking research to action. These collaborative research models combine "university knowledge" with "community knowledge." According to this model, both the methodological and theoretical knowledge of academic researchers and the practical knowledge of community members are essential components of effective research. The model also recognizes that community members and community organizations have a knowledge base and a practical understanding of the politics of social change that are often lacking on the academic side of this equation.

One cannot assume that this civically engaged research model is designed merely to help *citizens* become more effective agents of change as they seek to influence the social, economic, and political world around them. Rather, it is equally a matter of citizens helping *academic researchers* become more effective agents by informing them about how research methods, theory, and information can be put into play in the broader civic arena. This insight into collaborative university-community research is based on both direct research experience and the author's involvement in establishing a successful university-community collaborative research center that involves community partners at all stages of the research process—from conceptualization and research design to analysis, authorship, and dissemination of research outcomes.

PUBLIC SOCIOLOGY AND CIVIC ENGAGEMENT

While disciplines such as economics, political science, psychology, and social work have been highly visible in public arenas for decades, sociology has been more inconsistent in its embrace of connections to a broader civic world. On the one hand, sociology has sometimes worked to maintain an image of impartiality by keeping out of the fray of contemporary policy debates. In such cases, emphasis has been placed on disciplinary-based research priorities and publication in peer-reviewed journals. While their subject matter may be related to society and social institutions, some sociologists prefer to keep social change or policy reform efforts at arm's length for fear of being tainted as biased.

On the other hand, sociology is the quintessential field for understanding the complexities of social change, community life, and grassroots social movements. This is the field that produced Herbert Gans, a scholar who observed, lived among, and interviewed Italian American residents of Boston's North End in order to write *The Urban Villagers*.[1] Underneath a gritty urban exterior, he documented a tight-knit and functional community where city planners saw only social problems, urban decay, and fertile ground for developers to remove current residents and create a new, improved community. This 1962 study focused on displacement and gentrification processes before they became the subject of battles in urban communities across the country.

Other sociologists have authored policy reports, such as Daniel Moynihan's report on the destructive character of the social welfare system and James Coleman's report on the effects of educational investment on student achievement in public schools. While both reports set off controversies in local, regional, and national policy circles, they nonetheless represent a form of scholarship that addresses public issues in a critical and timely way. But these are examples of *policy* research done for a client; they do not necessarily represent a form of research that engages publics through back-and-forth debate in defining and completing the research.

Compared to other social science fields, sociology has been underrepresented even in policy research and has not been on the front lines of many policy battles. In the introduction of its report to the American Sociological Association Council, the ASA Task Force on Pubic Sociology cites the applied work of sociologists W. E. B. DuBois, Lester Ward, and Jane Adams, but then asks, "Why, 100 years after ASA's founding, is there a task force mandated to recommend methods for recognition and validation of on-going public sociology, guidelines for evaluating public sociology, and incentives and rewards for doing public sociology? This is because sociology as a discipline has never fully developed its promise to apply the tools and knowledge of sociology beyond the academy."[2]

Although sociologists have for decades worked collaboratively with members of community organizations and participants in social movements, their work has been marginalized by the field's professional association and by sociological journals. Moreover, the discipline's reward system does not generally encourage sociologists to venture far beyond discipline-bound scholarship into a more outwardly reaching civic-minded scholarship. In PhD-granting, research-oriented departments, tenure, promotion, and salary decisions are much more likely to be based on the number of publications in disciplinary-based journals than on the *impact* a sociologist's work has on current social problems or policy debates. Civic engagement—such as writing policy reports, completing evaluation research that measures the effectiveness of social programs, and publishing op-eds in local newspapers or articles in popular journals—is, at best, seen as "service" to the community.

The 2003 election of Michael Burawoy as president of the American Socio-logical Association marked a significant turning point for the field. Highly re-spected as a theorist, Burawoy framed sociological research aimed at broader non-academic audiences—and, in some cases, engaging broader segments of the public in the research—as "public sociology." This is a sociology rooted in past traditions and better connected to broader publics. In framing a new ap-proach to sociology based on strong civic involvement, Burawoy stated in his 2004 presidential address that the discipline

> has born its fruits. We have spent a century building professional knowledge, translating common sense into science, so that now, we are more than ready to embark on a systematic back-translation, taking knowledge back to those from whom it came, making public issues out of private troubles, and thus regenerat-ing sociology's moral fiber. Herein lies the promise and the challenge of public sociology, the complement and not the negation of professional sociology.[3]

While a part of public sociology maintains the traditional orientation whereby the expert studies the community and then tells the community what he or she has found, another part is oriented toward the co-creation of knowledge that is at the heart of civic studies. Burawoy described the role of the sociologist in an "organic" public sociology:

> [T]he sociologist works in close connection with a visible, thick, active, local and often counterpublic. The bulk of public sociology is indeed of an organic kind—sociologists working with a labor movement, neighborhood associations, communities of faith, immigrant rights groups, human rights organizations. Between the organic public sociologist and a public is a dialogue, a process of mutual education. The recognition of public sociology must extend to the or-ganic kind which often remains invisible, private, and is often considered to

be apart from our professional lives. The project of such public sociologies is to make visible the invisible, to make the private public, to validate these organic connections as part of our sociological life.[4]

What Burawoy calls "mutual education" is congruent with the idea of citizens as "creative agents" who work with experts and fellow citizens in understanding critical social problems and seeking active solutions to those problems. In fact, it is during this collaborative process that the ideological and practical boundaries of academic "expert" versus community "non-expert" naturally break down. In the everyday, organic process of engaging *with* publics on research, reflection, and social-change activities, a new consciousness and a new working arrangement between academic experts and citizen experts emerges.

THE LOYOLA UNIVERSITY CHICAGO CENTER
FOR URBAN RESEARCH AND LEARNING

To be more responsive to the needs and knowledge of civic audiences often overlooked or ignored by academic disciplines, the Loyola University Chicago founded the Center for Urban Research and Learning (CURL) in 1996. The creation of CURL predates the public sociology movement within the field. In fact, upon visiting CURL five years ago, Burawoy commented, "I only write about organic public sociology; you are doing it."[5] CURL is an innovative nontraditional urban research center that only conducts research projects that incorporate community organizations and agencies as collaborators at all stages—including the conceptualization and design of research methodologies, the collection and analysis of data, and the publication and dissemination of results.

Community involvement at the conceptualization stage is the most important part of the process. This is not a case of academics coming up with ideas for research and then asking community partners, "Do you want to join us?" Rather, conceptualization occurs through a back-and-forth between activists and practitioners, on the one hand, and researchers, on the other. This civically engaged process produces research projects that are different from those that would have been created by academic-based researchers alone.

For example, in its early years, CURL convened researchers and activists to explore alternatives to the segregation of communities that had characterized Chicago's history for decades. Related to this was the question of how to stop the cycle of gentrification and displacement, one of the processes that perpetuated segregation by displacing low-income families of color and replacing them with middle-class non-Hispanic white households. During the first two meetings, there was a lot of discussion about theories of gentrification/displacement and levels of segregation in Chicago and older cities in the Northeast and Midwest as measured by the "index of dissimilarity."[6]

It was during the third of these meeting that a collaborative university-community research epiphany occurred. In frustration, a community member said, "We don't care about more measures of how segregated our communities are. It doesn't make any difference whether Chicago is the most segregated city, the third-most segregated city, or the tenth-most segregated city. What we need are solutions to segregation. We have diverse communities in our city that have been diverse for 30 or 40 years. Why? What is going on there that is different from other seg-regated communities?"[7] This observation set off an extremely productive conver-sation that led to a two-year research project focused on what produces stable, diverse communities. CURL collected data on fourteen communities in nine cities using collaborative university-community teams in each city. A Chicago-based community partner was instrumental in getting funding from the US Department of Housing and Urban Development (HUD). The nine case studies and overview of the project were published as a dedicated issue of HUD's journal *Cityscape*.[8] This 1998 issue continues to serve as a guide for communities seeking to sustain diversity and break the cycle of segregation and re-segregation.

ADDING CHAIRS TO THE RESEARCH TABLE: CO-CREATING KNOWLEDGE
The kind of university-community collaboration described above brings com-munity partners and community knowledge into the research process. In essence, it "adds chairs" to the research table. For decades, academic researchers have used venues within the university and within various disciplines to debate issues, hone research approaches, and guide research. But there is no reason why community partners cannot be involved in all aspects of this process. The overall effect of the extra eyes, ears, and voices is to increase the quality of the individual researcher's work—whether he or she is participating in an active debate over the best survey questions to use in the course of an intradepartmental brown-bag lunch in the sociology department, or presenting a paper to colleagues at a national disci-plinary conference. This is not to say that university-community collaboration should be the only approach to research; rather, it is to say that collaborative research is an additional approach that can strengthen knowledge creation by involving a more varied collection of eyes, ears, and voices in the research process. There is nothing new about academic researchers looking at an issue from dif-ferent angles and perspectives; however, the unique contribution of collaborative research is to add a new range of community perspectives.

By working with community partners to frame research issues, most CURL research is naturally interdisciplinary. One of the disconnects between the university and the broader civic world is the mismatch between broad, holistic, inherently interdisciplinary issues in the community and the siloed environment in the university, where much is organized around separate schools and disciplines. Everyday citizen activities are not chopped up into the categories represented by academic disciplines. Similarly, problems and challenges in everyday civic life are not neatly divided into categories mirroring the siloed disciplines. Con-sequently, collaborative research is typically interdisciplinary research. While sociology, psychology, social work, and education constitute the core of much of CURL's research, faculty from law, political science, economics, communica-tions, philosophy, theology, nursing, medicine, criminal justice, environmental science, and other departments and schools have also been involved.

Since engaged research is the centerpiece of CURL's work, and since a variety of community organizations, social service organizations, and government agencies collaborate in the work of the center, the topics of CURL research cover many areas. For example, CURL conducted a three-year evaluation of the City of

Chicago's plan to end homelessness. Many public and private agencies that provide services to the homeless, along with a Chicago Alliance to End Homelessness "Consumers' Council" composed of users of various services for homeless individuals and families, helped inform the research process. In another CURL project, an economist and several sociology graduate students worked together to measure the impact of a new WalMart store on a low-income African American community in Chicago. Since this was only the second WalMart located in a city in the United States, much attention was focused on whether it would have a positive impact on sales tax revenues, employment, and business development.

Civically engaged research is not parochial research with a narrow scope. While much of CURL's research is community based, it often connects with regional, national, and even international policy. For example, a recent Ford Foundation project to assess the experience of undocumented students in American universities involved six university partners in five metropolitan areas and has served as the basis for more policy work by the foundation. An evaluation of the City of Chicago's Domestic Violence Help Line, which linked victims to agency and government support systems, has been used to create a new independent statewide network help line in Illinois. A current project is comparing residents' efforts to assert their own voices in low-income housing developments in Chicago and in Sydney, Australia.[9]

This civically engaged research has multiple characteristics that make it a dynamic process that adds energy and meaning to research process in ways that traditional research does not. There is typically a sense of urgency and immediacy to collaborative research. It typically addresses day-to-day problems and challenges facing individuals, families, or whole communities. While all involved recognize that any research project takes time, participants in collaborative research often display an impatience and a concern for reaching conclusions that keeps the research more focused than traditional academic research. Every day, every month, or every year that a problem lingers in a community is that much more time when people are hurt or are not able to realize opportunities to improve the quality of their lives. Traditional research does not always have such a sense of urgency. It is sometimes pushed aside during the busy times of the academic calendar or locked into multi-year schedules with few interim reports to local communities. With collaboration also comes a more organic relationship between research, policy, and social change. From the start, collaborative research is connected with a tangible problem in the community or a particular policy question—whether the research is being completed for one agency in the community or for a larger metropolitan network of agencies. From the first day of the research process, team members are thinking about how to shape the research in order to meet policy needs or influence activists' efforts to bring about positive changes. This is not an imperative felt in traditional academic research, which has only the immediate need of adding to knowledge in the discipline.

SOLUTION-ORIENTED RESEARCH
In contrast to the problem-oriented approach of most academic research, much collaborative research takes a solution-oriented approach. While community members are often motivated by a sense of urgency to *solve* problems, academic

researchers often spend an inordinate amount of time just describing problems. There is no question that one needs to understand the underlying causes of problems before crafting solutions. However, academic researchers often stop at the problems part of the process; connecting research to specific solutions or interventions is frequently seen as a "political" process, one in which an objective, unbiased researcher should not engage. Indeed, indicative of this traditional research orientation of the field is the fact that most sociology departments offer a course on "social problems." There are few, if any, sociology courses on "social solutions." Implicit in this is a boundary between academic research, on the one hand, and policy research and activism, on the other. By using research to understand *what is*, one can more comfortably appear to be objective and unbiased. However, when using the research process to describe *what could be*, a researcher can appear biased and inappropriately subjective.

There is an even more critical distinction between "solution-oriented" and "problem-oriented" research. Even within the field of civic studies, some may view engaged research as research that is conducted by academics who focus on community-defined issues. In essence, that is, the academic brings his or her expertise to bear on a community problem. This approach implies that *the community has a deficit* that needs to be corrected by the academic researcher, and it privileges the knowledge of the academic over that of the community leader or activist. Let us turn the tables on this approach to engaged research.

This "problem-oriented" approach—which assumes that the community has a deficit—obscures that fact that *academic researchers themselves may have a deficit* that needs to be corrected by experienced community leaders and activists. Academics may be well trained in methodology and theory, but they are not always trained or experienced in how to get things done—for example, to pressure elected officials to adopt new policies or to organize community opposition to a corporate policy perpetuating pollution in their neighborhoods. In contrast to a "problem-oriented" approach, a "solution-oriented" approach encompasses the research process of defining and understanding a problem *as well as the political process of bringing about change*. An individual who has been employed in a workplace setting for decades may understand the nuances of organizational structure and personalities and how they relate to power in the workplace. A seasoned community organizer may have learned over many years how to pull communities together and successfully put pressure on elected officials and elites who stand in the way of positive change. Indeed, it was academics' arrogant belief that their *problem*-oriented research approach should be central to any social change movement that prompted famed community-organizer Saul Alinsky to quip, "Asking a sociologist to solve a problem is like prescribing an enema for diarrhea."[10]

> *Academics may be well trained in methodology and theory, but they are not always trained or experienced in how to get things done, for example, to pressure elected officials to adopt new policies or to organize community opposition to a corporate policy perpetuating pollution in their neighborhoods*

It is the move into solution-oriented, "what-could-be" territory that distinguishes collaborative research from traditional research. The problem-oriented part of the research process—the identifying, describing, and understanding of social processes—is *one* step in this process. It is a *starting point*, rather than an endpoint. Forward-thinking, solution-oriented, engaged research involves taking the next step to map out how change can be accomplished. Although academic researchers do study the change process and can be knowledgeable about the "how-to" of social change, this second step necessarily calls more heavily on the knowledge and experience of citizens outside the academic research world. It is the organic collaboration between researcher and activist—the sharing of their respective knowledge bases and engagement with the tensions between their perspectives—that produces valuable, rigorous, civically engaged research. In civically engaged scholarship, researchers and citizen activists are equal partners.

Solution-oriented research also gives citizen activists more reason to participate in the research process. While the academic exercise of describing social processes and social problems may be of interest to some, it is the search for solutions that is particularly engaging to most community members. As the potential collective beneficiaries of engaged research, community members are likely to be willing partners in the pursuit of solutions.

Collaborative, solution-oriented research is also dynamic in that it unleashes the creativity that comes from crossing boundaries and includes a larger collectivity of people who bring perspectives, knowledge, and experiences that are different from those of the typical "lone-ranger" university researcher. The organic part of this boundary-crossing creates new research and activist communities where all participants increasingly understand the *need* to bring others into the research process, lest a critical dimension of a problem be missed or a potential solution ignored. Bringing academic researchers and citizen activists into the research process actually strengthens the quality of the process and its outcomes because it reduces the chance of missing key elements of research related to understanding problems and developing solutions. Here, the co-creation of knowledge is not only a matter of democratizing research, but it is also a matter of improving the rigor of research.

CONNECTING LOCAL COLLABORATIVE RESEARCH
TO NATIONAL AND INTERNATIONAL NETWORKS

The kind of grassroots-oriented, locally anchored research described above has often been undervalued in academic circles. The ability to generalize research outcomes beyond the local community or beyond the single case study has been important in academic disciplines. Traditionally, this has meant doing research that is coordinated or funded by a national or international agency, such as the National Science Foundation, the World Bank, or some other large organization. Regional, national, and international professional associations of disciplines have been well placed to take advantage of support from these funders. Local voices—the kind of citizen voices described above—are typically not a prominent part of this research beyond the local level.

However, new grassroots-anchored, regional, national, and international networks are emerging that bring together local, collaborative, researcher-activist centers. In part, these emerging networks are an outgrowth of a worldwide movement centered on community-based participatory research, participatory-action research, and university-community centers and networks. And in part, they are a product of cheaper and more accessible communication across regions and across nations. Most notably, access to the Internet and inexpensive telecommunications services has facilitated connections among a decentralized array of locally based research and social-change projects.

While CURL has been one of the larger and more visible collaborative university-community research centers, it is part of growing national and international networks of similar centers. For example, Campus Community Partners for Health (CCPH), one of the more visible and effective national networks in the public health field, has coordinated locally based but comparative national research projects on a variety of health issues. CCPH's biannual meeting serves as a networking space for researchers, policy makers, and community activists alike. CCPH has worked with other organizations to bring citizens' voices into the research process by promoting community-based participatory research in university environments, working to expand the definition of scholarly work in tenure reviews to include community-based research, and promoting the formation of non-university research review boards in order to strengthen the control of community residents and community-based organizations over the research enterprise in local communities.

In Europe, a network of "science shops"—typically university-based research and service centers working with local communities—has existed since the 1970s. Partially supported with funding from the European Union (EU), the Living-Knowledge network has nearly doubled in size since its formation, and now includes more than thirty "science shops" across the EU. Through its biannual conference, LivingKnowledge provides opportunities for members to connect with other collaborative research networks around the world. The conference is typically attended by grassroots researchers from Africa, Latin America, Asia, North America, and Australia.

The Global Alliance on Community-Engaged Research (GACER) is a Canada-based network with connections to other grassroots networks in more than fourteen countries. In 2008, six hundred attendees at an international GACER conference endorsed a *Declaration of the Global Alliance* that states that engagement in civically engaged research is an issue of human rights. The declaration presents such research as part of "the right to learn, the right to know, the right to produce knowledge, and the right to access knowledge" as defined and protected by the 1948 United Nations *Universal Declaration of Human Rights*.[11]

New electronic journals, virtual networks, and blogs have also created direct connections among local researcher-activist networks—connections that do not have to be moderated by national and international agencies. For example, in cooperation with the University of Technology Sydney Shopfront, a collaborative university-community research center, CURL now publishes *Gateways: An International Journal of Community Research and Engagement.* With over three thousand readers in thirty countries, *Gateways* publishes peer-reviewed research articles that report on a variety of community-based projects. However, unlike disciplinary journals, *Gateways* defines "peer" to include not just academics, but also non-academics with direct knowledge and experience related to the communities that are the subjects of the research.

A MORE CIVICALLY-CENTERED ENTERPRISE:
ORGANIC PUBLIC SOCIOLOGY, ENGAGED RESEARCH, AND CIVIC STUDIES
Many of the components of a democratic, grassroots-anchored, civic studies research paradigm already exist. Part of the task ahead is to elevate the role of the citizen as co-creator of knowledge, both inside and outside academia. The task also involves getting academic researchers to understand that they, too, have knowledge deficits when it comes to understanding community politics and identifying potentially successful strategies for social change at the grassroots level. Whether it is the "new" organic public sociology (along with participatory research networks in many other fields) or the already established working relationships among university researchers and grassroots activists, a rich body of theoretical, practical, and organizational knowledge already exists and can serve as a foundation upon which to establish civic studies.

As with researcher-activist collaboration itself, the creation of an explicitly democratic field of civic studies is a political process. On the one hand, it challenges business as usual in academic worlds where peer review is the gold standard of research and "citizen voice" and solution-oriented research are seen as abandonments of research objectivity. On the other hand, it involves a cadre of civic studies researchers and citizen activists working together in order to make the case for new approaches that bring everyday citizens into the research process—approaches that give broader publics a voice in the research process.

The academic side of the project to create a field of civic studies will involve taking advantage of the new doors that have opened to community-based research in various disciplines. Because civically engaged research is not bound by disciplines, but rather is defined by the need to seek practical solutions to community problems, this effort is certainly interdisciplinary. On the community side, many university-community research networks, centers, and alliances have already engaged thousands of community leaders in rigorous, activist, collaborative, solution-oriented research. The foundation has been built to support a new, more inclusive research enterprise.

NOTES
1. Gans, *The Urban Villagers* (New York: Free Press, 1962).
2. American Sociological Association Task Force on Institutionalizing Public Sociology, *Public Sociology and the Roots of American Sociology: Re-establishing Our Connections to the Public* (Washington, DC: American Sociological Association, 2005), 1.
3. Burawoy, "2004 Presidential Address: For Public Sociology," *American Sociological Review* 70, no. 1 (2005): 4–28.
4. Ibid., 7–8.
5. Burawoy, in discussion with the author, February, 2008.
6. The index of dissimilarity is a standard measure of segregation used by researchers to determine how many members of particular racial or ethnic groups would have to move in order to produce

a non-segregated city. Typically, the findings are reported as comparisons of racial or ethnic groups—black/white comparisons, for example, or non-Hispanic white/Hispanic comparisons.

7. Community participant, Policy Research and Action Group Working Group on Racial Segregation, February 1996.

8. P. Nyden, J. Lukehart, M. Maly, and W. Peterman, eds., "Racially and Ethnically Diverse Communities," special issue, *Cityscape: A Journal of Policy Development and Research* 4, no. 2 (1998).

9. More information about these and other CURL projects, including the outcomes and reports of research efforts, can be found online at http://www.luc.edu/curl/research.shtml.

10. S. Alinsky, "Interview with Saul Alinsky, Feisty Radical Organizer," *Playboy* 19, no. 3 (March 1972), 59.

11. Global Alliance on Community-Engaged Research, *Declaration of the Global Alliance* (Victoria, BC: Global Alliance on Community-Engaged Research, 2008), http://www.gacer.org/pdf/Global-Alliance-Declaration_May-2008.pdf.

Contributors

Paul Dragos Aligica, Senior Research Fellow, F. A. Hayek Program for Advanced Study in Philosophy, Politics and Economics, George Mason University

Harry C. Boyte, Director, Center for Democracy and Citizenship, Augsburg College; Senior Fellow, Humphrey School of Public Affairs, University of Minnesota

Peter Levine, Lincoln Filene Professor of Citizenship & Public Affairs and Director, Center for Information & Research on Civic Learning & Engagement, Jonathan M. Tisch College of Citizenship and Public Service, Tufts University

Ghazala Mansuri, Lead Economist, Poverty Reduction and Equity Group and Development Research Group, The World Bank

Greg Munno, Ph.D. Candidate, S.I. Newhouse School of Public Communication, Syracuse University

Tina Nabatchi, Associate Professor, Department of Public Administration and International Affairs, Maxwell School of Citizenship and Public Affairs, Syracuse University

Philip Nyden, Professor of Sociology and Director, the Center for Urban Research and Learning, Loyola University Chicago

Vijayendra Rao, Lead Economist, Development Research Group, The World Bank

Filippo Sabetti, Professor, Department of Political Science, McGill University

Blase Scarnati, Director, First and Second Year Learning and Co-Director, First Year Learning Initiative, Northern Arizona University

Sanford F. Schram, Professor, Department of Political Science, Hunter College, CUNY

Karol Edward Sołtan, Associate Professor of Government and Politics, University of Maryland at College Park; Co-Director and Co-founder of the Summer Institute of Civic Studies at Tufts University

Bringing
Theory to
Practice

Bringing Theory to Practice is an independent project in partnership with the Association of American Colleges and Universities, and supported by the S. Engelhard Center (whose major contributors include the Charles Engelhard Foundation and the Christian A. Johnson Endeavor Foundation, in addition to other foundations and individuals).

Bringing Theory to Practice (BTtoP) encourages colleges and universities to assert their core purposes as educational institutions not only to advance learning and discovery, but also to advance the potential and well-being of each student as a whole person, and to advance education as a public good that sustains a civic society.

BTtoP supports campus-based initiatives that demonstrate how uses of engaged forms of learning that actively involve students, both within and beyond the classroom, can directly contribute to their cognitive, emotional, and civic development. The work of the project is conducted primarily through sponsored research, conferences, grants to colleges and universities of all types, and publications—notably including *Transforming Undergraduate Education: Theory that Compels and Practices that Succeed,* edited by Donald W. Harward (Lanham, MD: Rowman & Littlefield, 2012.).

BTtoP provides a rare source of intellectual and practical assistance to all institutional constituencies that are seeking to make or strengthen the changes needed to realize their own missions of learning and discovery, and that are working to create campus cultures for learning that recognize the necessary connections among higher learning and students' well-being and civic engagement.

Information about current grant opportunities, project publications, and forthcoming conferences is available online at **www.BTtoP.org**.